This book should be essential among others. The authors, b way about how to plan to stuc of study to prepare for evaluations. Reading this book will prepare students to master various types of subject matter in any level of education.

—**HENRY L. ROEDIGER, III, PhD,** JAMES S. McDONNELL DISTINGUISHED UNIVERSITY PROFESSOR OF PSYCHOLOGY, WASHINGTON UNIVERSITY IN ST. LOUIS, ST. LOUIS, MO

Regan Gurung and John Dunlosky, two leaders in the field of how people learn and what they can do to make learning last, have written a gem of a book for everyone who wants learning to be easier, more effective, and longer lasting. This book will pay lifelong dividends for everyone who wants to learn.

—**DIANE F. HALPERN, PhD,** PROFESSOR EMERITA, CLAREMONT McKENNA COLLEGE, CLAREMONT, CA

This is the perfect book to help undergraduate students learn to learn without excess baggage. The book is clear, concise, and focused, and the authors—two scholar–teachers—write in an engaging, accessible style that will help readers master practices and strategies that really do work. Teachers of introductory-level courses: Take note!

—**DANA S. DUNN, PhD,** PROFESSOR OF PSYCHOLOGY, MORAVIAN UNIVERSITY, BETHLEHEM, PA

STUDY
LIKE A CHAMP

THE Psychology-Based Guide TO "Grade A" Study Habits

STUDY LIKE A CHAMP

Regan A. R. Gurung PHD
John Dunlosky PHD

 AMERICAN PSYCHOLOGICAL ASSOCIATION

Published by
APA LifeTools
750 First Street, NE
Washington, DC 20002
https://www.apa.org

Order Department
https://www.apa.org/pubs/books
order@apa.org

In the U.K., Europe, Africa, and the Middle East, copies may be ordered from Eurospan
https://www.eurospanbookstore.com/apa
info@eurospangroup.com

Typeset in Sabon by Circle Graphics, Inc., Reisterstown, MD

Printer: Sheridan Books, Chelsea, MI
Cover Designer: Mark Karis

Library of Congress Cataloging-in-Publication Data

Names: Gurung, Regan A. R. author. | Dunlosky, John, author.
Title: Study like a champ : the psychology-based guide to "grade A" study habits / Regan A.R. Gurung and John Dunlosky.
Description: Washington, DC : American Psychological Association, [2023] | Includes bibliographical references and index.
Identifiers: LCCN 2022027877 (print) | LCCN 2022027878 (ebook) | ISBN 9781433840173 (paperback) | ISBN 9781433840180 (ebook)
Subjects: LCSH: Study skills. | Educational psychology. | Learning, Psychology of. | BISAC: STUDY AIDS / Study & Test-Taking Skills | JUVENILE NONFICTION / Study Aids / General
Classification: LCC LB1049 .G84 2023 (print) | LCC LB1049 (ebook) | DDC 371.30281--dc23/eng/20220713
LC record available at https://lccn.loc.gov/2022027877
LC ebook record available at https://lccn.loc.gov/2022027878

https://doi.org/10.1037/0000327-000

Printed in the United States of America

10 9 8 7 6 5 4 3 2

To students everywhere who tackle the complexities of learning, expend the effort to improve, and maintain the motivation to keep going in the face of challenges. May the tools of psychological science boost your endeavors to championship levels.

CONTENTS

PREFACE

OR WHY YOU SHOULD REALLY CARE ABOUT WHAT'S IN THIS BOOK

If you want to know the best way to learn, this book is for you.

Study Like a Champ provides you with the answer to the oft-asked question "What can I do to get an A?" We take years of psychological research on how learning works and what strategies best help one learn, and we translate the results into easy-to-understand, pragmatic—and, most important—easy-to-follow tips. But that's not all.

We have watched and listened as our students have tried to study better. We have seen students read other books on how to study yet still not improve. Part of the reason why is that it is easy for scientists and instructors to tell you what to do, but it is a whole other thing to actually be able to do it. So, we looked for reasons why students have trouble following guidance on how to study and have come up with some hacks to help. We also show you evidence to support our recommendations. We want you to know what to do and why to do it.

Furthermore, we show you which strategies work best for learning different kinds of material. Not every class is the same. What it takes to do well in an introductory psychology class may not be the same as what it takes to do well in a computer science class. We have your back.

This guide was written by expert psychology teachers who also conduct the very research on which the tips are based. You are in good hands. Collectively, we have published more than 200 research articles on the very material we share with you. We invite you behind the curtain so you can see the secrets of research conducted both in laboratories as well as in classrooms. However, although we are well versed in writing for peer-reviewed research journals, we wrote this book for you, dear student, not for academic researchers. This book is designed to be useful for every college student who wants to know how to learn well.

We recognize that many instructors do not spend much time teaching students how to learn. Many college faculty either believe students have learned how to learn either in high school or in a University 101–type course, or they do not believe it is their job to teach learning skills. In other cases, faculty may share suggestions about the best ways to study (e.g., "Make sure you spread out your studying," "Make sure you test yourself") but do not share exactly how to follow the advice; nor do they reward optimal study habits. Even hardworking students often believe that it is the amount of time that they study, not exactly how they use that time to study, that is most important. We wrote this book to address these issues head on—to explain how to schedule your study time and exactly what to do when you sit down to study.

We also want to demystify the cognitive science behind how people learn, and thus we provide simple, classroom-tested tools to begin and maintain habits that will foster lifelong learning. We want you to be a Study Champion; accordingly, we provide clear steps on how to plan, monitor, and evaluate your learning with easy-to-follow instructions. In essence, we first explain what to do, and then we show why each step matters. This is not a textbook; it is your training manual to become a Study Champion.

OUR ORIGIN STORY

At one time, we were both graduate students at the University of Washington in Seattle. We were not the same age as we are now, and we definitely did not have the same length of hair back then; John evidently did not understand what a barber was for. Regan remembers his first sight of John as being a blur of hair flying by as John strode down the corridor to his lab past Regan's office. John is a cognitive psychologist. Regan is a social psychologist. We both love trying to understand what makes people learn better. After graduate school, we went in two different directions: both literally, in terms of geography, and figuratively, in terms of our research interests.

Fast-forward a sizable number of years. We were both successful researchers and established teachers and noticed that so much good science was available *about* learning, but so little of it focused on how to explain the science to students. Sometimes instructors would tell students what to do in one class, but most of the faculty we talked with shared that they focused more on content in their classes and did not share how their students should best learn the content. And, after all, many faculty (who are not experts on cognition) have misconceptions about learning!

A FEW KEY ACKNOWLEDGMENTS

We decided to take action. We began by looking at the different books on studying already out there and felt we had something new and different to say. We got some early support from Eric Landrum and Christine Cardone, who thought this was a great idea and urged us to surge forward. Christine also read through early versions of these chapters and provided some helpful feedback. We appreciate it. We were met with great enthusiasm by another Chris, Christopher Kelaher, at American Psychological Association Books, who signed us to a contract and got this book into production in record time. Beth Hatch was a supportive and eagle-eyed development editor, and three reviewers provided critical points for us to ponder in creating the final version. A special shout-out goes to Paige Herrboldt, who created all the end-of-chapter artwork especially for this book.

Both of us are inspired by our students and by a passion to share psychological science with them and now with you. Many of the examples in this book come from real student questions, comments, and outbursts. Yes, we got some ideas from Instagram memes and college TikTok videos as well.

We would also like to thank our partners in particular for their support. In addition, we were aided by the company of one very cute cat, Haki (John), and darling dog, Katsu (Regan).

I

GROUNDWORK

CHAPTER 1

SO YOU THINK YOU KNOW HOW TO STUDY? LET'S FoK ABOUT IT

In this chapter, you will learn

- why you may not really know what you think you know,
- major myths about learning, and
- the key factors that predict learning.

To be a champion learner, you need look no further than what makes athletes champions. Kayla, one of our students, is a champion gymnast. She is also a champion student with a straight 4.0 grade point average, the quintessential student–athlete. If you ask her how she became a champion, Kayla will tell you two elements are key: Know what to do, and then practice—a lot. It also pays to have great coaches. We are here to help with the coaching part and show you what to do. Although we do not claim greatness (we are modest), not only have we been coaching students on how to study for years, but we also have done the research exploring *how* to be a Study Champion. Join us, and you too can be a Study Champion. You will know exactly what to do. We will show you how to do it. All you need to do is practice.

Most students coming to college have a set way of doing things. After all, "studying" is pretty straightforward, right? You go to class, take notes, get the book, read it, maybe reread it, then read your notes, make flash cards and interact with them a night or two before the exam, and then you are ready, right? Whereas some students do not do all of the activities in the last sentence, many do, and use additional strategies as well. But are these the best ways to study? You might be surprised to learn what the research says.

Be prepared to be shocked. We know you may already have your favorite study techniques. After all, parents and teachers always tell you how to study. Are your study habits good ones? You will find out the answer to this question as you read on. We will share the most effective approaches to studying like a champion.

In the next eight chapters, we provide solutions to study challenges, such as how to best use flash cards, and many others as well. Our goal is to highlight various ways that students study and point out which ways really are not so effective, but, most important, we highlight those that work well and describe in detail how to use them with fidelity.

WAIT, WHAT ABOUT "FoK ABOUT IT"?

The subtitle of this chapter is not an obscenity. Yes, we evoke the retort FUGGETABOUT it while we pun about talking about studying. The term is perhaps at the heart of what determines how much effort you put into studying and whether you stop. We all think we know how to study, and most of us are doing something right as long as we are doing something at all.

The first challenge when studying is to get a good sense of what you know and what you do not. Cognitive scientists call this the *feeling of knowing* (FoK). For every class, assignment, or topic, you have a FoK. Sometimes the FoK is strong, and you really believe you know the course material. The bad news? Your FoKs are often unreliable indicators of whether you really do know something. But before we overview some major myths about learning, let's take a look at what you already may know. Remember, it is always a good idea to first establish what you already know before facing new information.

The following survey was developed for a research project on study habits (Bartoszewski & Gurung, 2015).

Start Now: How Are Your Study Habits?

Think about your most challenging class. Now answer each of the questions that follow in regard to how you study for that class. For each question, indicate the extent to which you agree or disagree using the following scale: *Strongly Disagree* = 1, *Disagree* = 2, *Somewhat Disagree* = 3, *Somewhat Agree* = 4, *Strongly Agree* = 5.

I. Please think about how you utilize highlighting/underlining when marking potentially important portions of to-be-learned materials while reading.

1. ______ Within an assigned reading, I highlight or underline information.
2. ______ I frequently highlight or underline the information within one page.
3. ______ I prefer to use or study material in an assigned reading that has been previously highlighted or underlined by a previous user.
4. ______ I look at or use the material I previously highlighted or underlined within a given week.
5. ______ I find highlighting or underlining information in an assigned reading useful.

II. Please think about writing summaries (of various lengths) of to-be-learned texts.

1. ______ After assigned readings, I write summaries on the previous read material.
2. ______ After lectures, I write summaries on the information discussed.
3. ______ I am assigned to write summaries on lecture or reading materials.
4. ______ I find writing summaries of recently learned materials useful.

III. Please think about using key words and mental imagery to associate verbal materials.

1. ______ I associate key words with mental imagery to learn verbal material.
2. ______ I use the strategy of associating key words with mental imagery in relation to verbal material when taking an exam.
3. ______ I find using key words and mental imagery to associate verbal materials useful.

IV. Please think about attempting to form mental images of text materials while reading or listening.

1. ______ I form mental images of text materials while reading or listening.
2. ______ I recall mental images of text images that were formed while reading or listening on an exam.
3. ______ I find forming mental images of text materials while reading or listening useful.

V. Please think about restudying text material again after an initial reading.

1. ______ I go back to reread the information I did not comprehend.
2. ______ I go back to reread assigned readings when preparing for an exam.
3. ______ I am able to recall information that I have reread when taking an exam.
4. ______ I am able to understand the text material after the second time of rereading the initial reading.
5. ______ I find rereading information that I have previously read useful.

VI. Please think about implementing a schedule of practice that mixes different kinds of problems, or a schedule of study that mixes different kinds of material, within a single study session.

1. ______ I mix different kinds of problems within a single study session.
2. ______ I study different kinds of material within a single study session.

3. ______ I find using practice that mixes different kinds of problems within a single study session useful.
4. ______ I find studying different kinds of materials within a single study session useful.

VII. Please think about generating an explanation for why an explicitly stated fact or concept is true.

1. ______ I create an explanation for why a straightforward fact or concept is true.
2. ______ I am confident that creating an explanation for why a straightforward fact or concept is true helps me with learning the specific material.
3. ______ I find creating an explanation for why a straightforward fact or concept is true useful.

VIII. Please think about explaining how new information is related to known information in class or explaining steps taken during problem solving.

1. ______ I relate new information to previously known information.
2. ______ I explain the steps taken during problem solving.
3. ______ I am able to recall the new information I related to previously known information during an exam.
4. ______ I am able to recall the steps I have taken during problem solving during an exam.
5. ______ I find explaining how new information is related to known information useful.
6. ______ I find explaining steps taken during problem solving useful.
7. ______ I am confident that relating new information to previously known information helps me learn the material.
8. ______ I am confident that explaining the steps taken during problem solving helps me learn the material.

IX. Please think about self-testing or taking practice tests over to-be-learned material.

1. ______ I often self-test myself on the material learned in class within a given week.
2. ______ I take quizzes for my class within a given week.

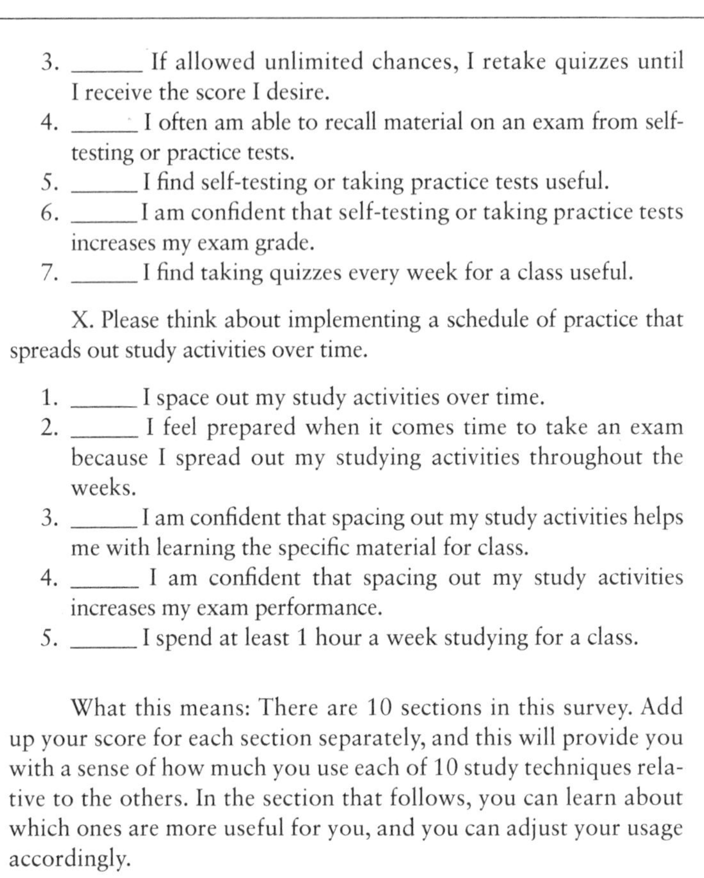

3. ______ If allowed unlimited chances, I retake quizzes until I receive the score I desire.
4. ______ I often am able to recall material on an exam from self-testing or practice tests.
5. ______ I find self-testing or taking practice tests useful.
6. ______ I am confident that self-testing or taking practice tests increases my exam grade.
7. ______ I find taking quizzes every week for a class useful.

X. Please think about implementing a schedule of practice that spreads out study activities over time.

1. ______ I space out my study activities over time.
2. ______ I feel prepared when it comes time to take an exam because I spread out my studying activities throughout the weeks.
3. ______ I am confident that spacing out my study activities helps me with learning the specific material for class.
4. ______ I am confident that spacing out my study activities increases my exam performance.
5. ______ I spend at least 1 hour a week studying for a class.

What this means: There are 10 sections in this survey. Add up your score for each section separately, and this will provide you with a sense of how much you use each of 10 study techniques relative to the others. In the section that follows, you can learn about which ones are more useful for you, and you can adjust your usage accordingly.

TEN THINGS WE THOUGHT WE KNEW (THAT ARE WRONG)

Throughout this book, we highlight many different myths. The key is to not let these unproven and sometimes wrong beliefs about learning hamper your own studying. The following are some of the biggest myths (De Bruyckere et al., 2015):

1. People have different styles of learning that are relevant to how they should be effectively taught or study.
2. Learning effectiveness can be illustrated in a pyramid.
3. You learn most informally (70%), then from others (20%), and then from formal education (10%).
4. Having knowledge is not important because you can look everything up.
5. Knowledge is as perishable as fresh fish.
6. You learn better if you discover things for yourself (vs. having it explained to you by others).
7. You can learn effectively through problem-based education.
8. Boys are naturally better at math than are girls.
9. In education, you need to take account of different types of intelligence.
10. Our memory records exactly what we experience.

You have probably heard of many of these myths. The one that really makes most faculty squirm is the first one, which perhaps is the most common misunderstanding about learning (Weinstein et al., 2018). Many people believe they learn better when they are taught in a style that matches their most preferred learning style. For instance, if they prefer to learn with visuals, or "by doing," their instructors should teach them with either visuals or experience, respectively. However, the data say otherwise. In a major review of studies that examined this issue, Pashler and colleagues (2008) concluded that the best instructional method involves different styles and that a match between learning and teaching style is not important. Share that the next time someone tells you they wish their instructor taught in a way that matches their style.

The learning-style issue is just the tip of the iceberg; there are many other myths out there. Our second major peeve relates to the *learning pyramid*, also known as the *cone of learning*, shown in

Figure 1.1. The model was supposedly developed by the National Training Laboratories Institute in the early 1960s, but the exact details are hard to come by. Although it is commonly shared as a meme on social media, it is inaccurate and portrays major misunderstandings of how we learn. This figure has no factual basis, so pay it no heed.

Many instructors who use the learning pyramid as a guide feel pressure to lecture less, fearing that it would lead to less learning. First, remember there can be great lectures and bad lectures. Any technique or technology, for that matter, can be used poorly. We are sure you have experienced some dull and boring ones too, but we hope you also have experienced great lecturers. In fact, any of the techniques in the learning pyramid can be used well or poorly.

FIGURE 1.1. A Commonly Shared Meme on Social Media That Is Inaccurate and Portrays Major Misunderstandings of How We Learn

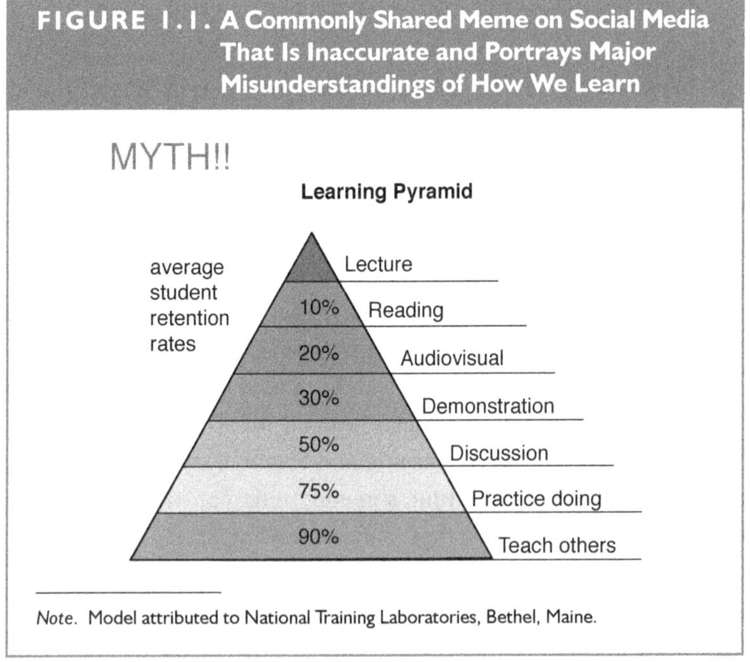

Note. Model attributed to National Training Laboratories, Bethel, Maine.

Although active learning can be effective (Bernstein, 2018), there are many varieties of it, such as group work and problem solving out loud, that are not always effective and can undermine your learning. Most important, the numbers in Figure 1.1 do not come from any solid research. On closer examination, those numbers were found to be mere approximations and guesstimates (De Bruyckere et al., 2015). So, do not panic, because your learning will not suffer if you do not have a chance to "teach others" or "practice doing," although in some circumstances these approaches can be useful.

You cannot blame yourself for believing many of the myths we listed earlier. In fact, a study of teacher training programs in the United States showed that 59% of programs do not mention any key principles of learning that are based on strong experimental research from cognitive psychology (Pomerance et al., 2016). Moreover, inaccurate findings related to learning are so common and widespread that some researchers deem them urban myths (De Bruyckere et al., 2015). Social media makes it easier to share an infographic of a myth than to educate students on the realities of learning. How much can you do with a 140-character tweet, anyway? Even if you do read the research on education, you still may not know what to believe. To see why, take a look at the two summaries of what works and what does not work for learning shown in Exhibit 1.1.

See anything interesting? Even if you were never good at those spot-the-differences puzzles, you should have noticed that both table columns list the same items. That is because one study may find that using a certain method (e.g., group learning) is useful, whereas another study did not find the same outcome. This is a good reason why you should be critical about what you read and have a basic working knowledge of research methods. Some types of research studies are more robust than others. For example, if you see the

EXHIBIT 1.1. Conflicting Results

What helps learning, according to research	What does NOT help learning, according to research
Traditional lecture	Traditional lecture
Active learning	Active learning
Service learning	Service learning
Problem-based learning	Problem-based learning
Group learning	Group learning
Mentoring	Mentoring
Cooperative learning	Cooperative learning
Discovery learning	Discovery learning
Inductive learning	Inductive learning
Learning by example	Learning by example
Interteaching	Interteaching
Desirable difficulty	Desirable difficulty
Learner-centered instruction	Learner-centered instruction
Curriculum-centered learning	Curriculum-centered learning
Online teaching	Online teaching
Clickers	Clickers
PowerPoint presentations	PowerPoint presentations
Overheads	Overheads
Chalktalks	Chalktalks
Teachable moments	Teachable moments
Universal design of instruction	Universal design of instruction
Multiple intelligences	Multiple intelligences
Kolb's learning styles	Kolb's learning styles
Journaling	Journaling
Reflective practice	Reflective practice
Reciprocal teaching	Reciprocal teaching
Uncoverage	Uncoverage
Concept maps	Concept maps
Question generation	Question generation
Film strips	Film strips
Laboratory-based instruction	Laboratory-based instruction

EXHIBIT 1.1. Conflicting Results (*Continued*)

What helps learning, according to research	What does NOT help learning, according to research
Video clips	Video clips
Role playing	Role playing
Modeling	Modeling
Programmed instruction	Programmed instruction
Keller method	Keller method
Skill practice	Skill practice
Guided practice	Guided practice
Collaborative learning	Collaborative learning
Apprenticeship	Apprenticeship
Situated learning	Situated learning
Authentic assessment	Authentic assessment
Formative assessment	Formative assessment
Classroom research techniques	Classroom research techniques
Book reports	Book reports
Class discussion	Class discussion
Small-group discussion	Small-group discussion
Think–pair–share	Think–pair–share
Peer instruction	Peer instruction
Concept tests	Concept tests
Panel of experts	Panel of experts
Brainstorming	Brainstorming
Case studies	Case studies
Worksheets	Worksheets
Guest speakers	Guest speakers

Note. Copyright by Steven Chew. Adapted with permission.

word "meta-analysis," you should pay more attention because meta-analyses are studies that combine a lot of different study results together and are therefore the strongest examples of scientific evidence. Figure 1.2 shows the hierarchy of scientific evidence, with the strongest evidence on top.

Evaluating research, however, is not what this book is about. We have sifted through the research for you. When we give you study tips in this book, you can rest assured that our tips are based on the most robust studies available.

FIGURE 1.2. Hierarchy of Scientific Evidence

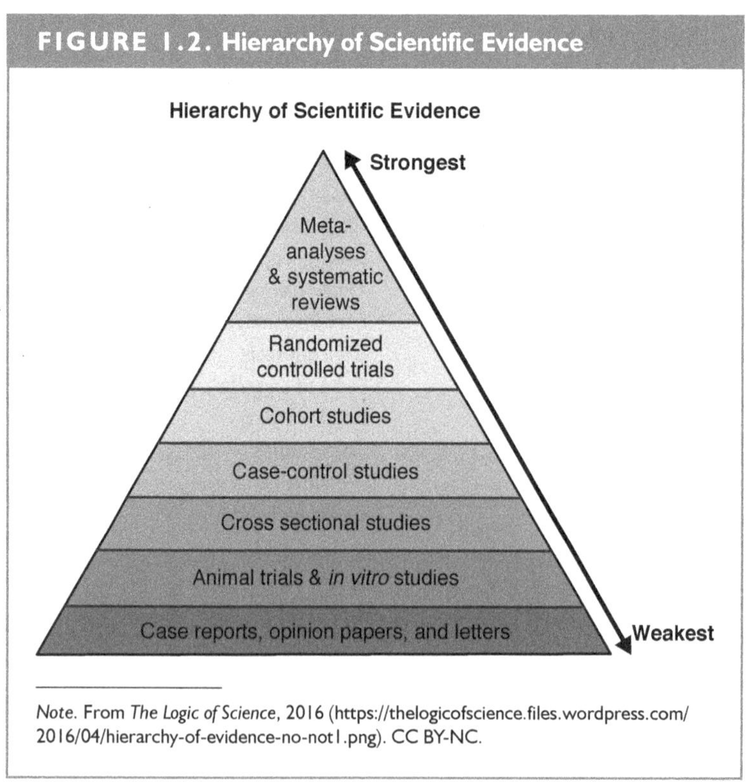

Note. From *The Logic of Science*, 2016 (https://thelogicofscience.files.wordpress.com/2016/04/hierarchy-of-evidence-no-not1.png).

WHAT IS METACOGNITION?

One thing we know from an abundance of research is that to study like a champion, your major goal is to improve your metacognitive abilities. *Metacognition* is thinking about your thinking. When you consciously look at what you know and what you do not know, and try to change your thought processes, you are doing metacognitive work. People have a wide range of automatic thoughts about and reactions to everyday activities. When you approach learning, you automatically use the same strategies you have used for years without necessarily examining what you are doing. We human beings do not always use the most effective ways to think, and we often have unhealthy ways of thinking. Although fascinating areas of study include why people have biased, inflated, or negative views of themselves, those are not the types of thoughts we address in this book. It is true that sometimes our FoKs are inflated too, and those are the kind of thoughts with which we concern ourselves.

> *When you consciously look at what you know, what you do not know, and try to change your thought processes, you are doing metacognitive work.*

Metacognition has been a major area of focus in cognitive study since John Flavell (1979) first coined the term. For obvious reasons, examinations of metacognition are a major part of research done on cognition and education because it involves many critical functions, such as being consciously aware of oneself as a problem solver and the ability to accurately judge one's level of learning. You are not reading this book to learn about research on metacognition, but if you want to know more, you may want to check out Dunlosky and Rawson's (2019) book, which features reviews of studies of reading, note taking, planning, and more.

In the chapters to come, we cover three distinct parts of metacognition as they pertain to learning and studying. First, you need to be able to better *plan* out your learning. Next, you need to *monitor* your learning, paying attention to what you know and what you do not know. Finally, you need to *revise* your plan according to your assessment of your learning. The major cognitive strategies that are part of studying like a champion involve these three elements of metacognition, and knowing which strategies are most effective is also an aspect of metacognition because it concerns your knowledge about how your mind works and learns.

BEING A STUDY CHAMPION: AN OVERVIEW

Research has uncovered many variables that influence how well you learn (Komarraju & Nadler, 2013; Robbins et al., 2004). Here are some of the factors most frequently discussed in the educational psychology literature (Gurung, 2016):

- motivation
- habits
- ability
- effort
- self-efficacy
- social support
- goals

These factors are not surprising. Of course, you need to work hard, care about your learning and scores, and have goals and good study habits. You should also make sure you have a positive mindset that includes believing that intelligence is flexible, not fixed (Dweck, 2007). Although many of these predictors of learning seem obvious, others are not discussed as often. Two somewhat surprising ones are social support and self-efficacy (i.e., the belief that you can successfully accomplish something). Many teachers may not give the value of support and rapport enough credit, but clearly they are key components of successful learning. In a major Gallup–Purdue study of successful college students, 63% of the more than 30,000 students sampled said that having at least one professor who made them excited about learning was critical to their success (Gallup, Inc., 2014). Feeling that teachers cared, and having a mentor who encouraged them to pursue goals and dreams, were also deemed important.

Might there be other significant factors, even if they are not discussed as frequently as the ones just mentioned? Which factors are really the most important? John Hattie (2015) took a close look at more than 65,000 studies of student achievement. Together, the studies involved close to a quarter of a billion students. Yes: 250,000,000. He did complex meta-analyses and used a handy statistical indicator called an *effect size*, which allows you to get a strong sense of just how important a certain factor is. The higher the effect size, the more important the factor (and thus it's a great statistic to look for when you read about research, even in social media).

Hattie created a table that listed the top 195 factors that influence learning. The most important factors to blame (with low or negative effect sizes) included depression and television watching. Some important factors to praise (those with positive effect sizes) included teacher estimates of student achievement, teacher efficacy, study skills, and classroom discussion. Class size? Not a big deal. Single-sex schools, gender, or type of testing? Next to no effect. Wait: It gets better.

Hattie then did something that saved a lot of us a lot of time. He combined all the data from all the different studies and looked for common groupings of factors that influenced learning. The goal was to pinpoint the factors most responsible for learning. Hattie's work suggests that the lion's share—near half—of what predicts learning is how you approach studying. The next largest single chunk of influence was teacher qualities. What teachers do, their training, their characteristics, account for 20% to 25% of the variance in learning (see Figure 1.3). The rest can be attributed to your peers (5%), home factors (5%), and a number of other smaller contributors. The most important finding for our purpose is this: Half of learning depends on what you do.

So, if students' study habits are 50% of the deal, which study habits are the most effective? In perhaps the most in-depth review of study techniques to date, Dunlosky et al. (2013) rated the effectiveness of 10 learning techniques that are all free to use and (at least

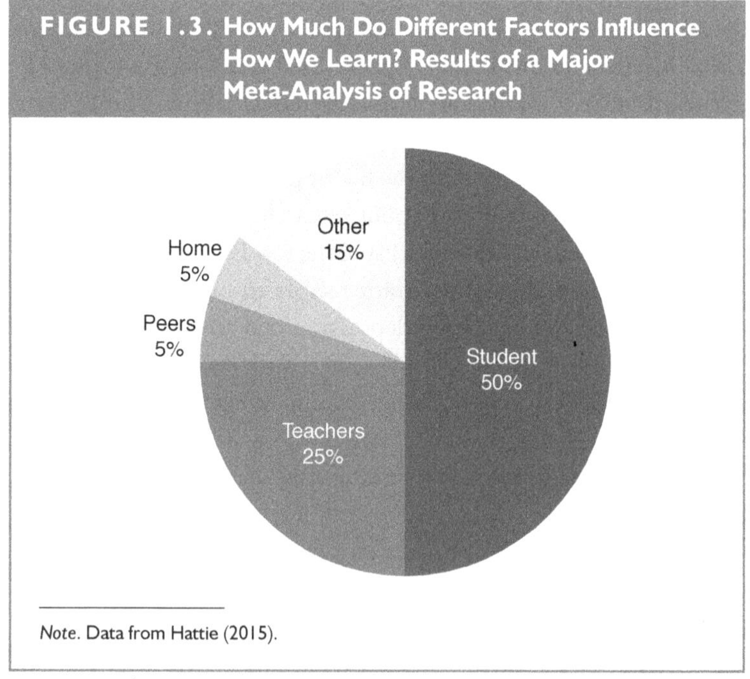

FIGURE 1.3. How Much Do Different Factors Influence How We Learn? Results of a Major Meta-Analysis of Research

Note. Data from Hattie (2015).

some) are often used by students. They also rated the techniques' *utility*, or practical usefulness, on the basis of the extent to which the technique would apply to different learners, classes, content, exams, and educational settings. All 10 techniques are listed and defined in Table 1.1 (and in the Glossary at the end of the book). All 10 can improve learning, although they vary in utility. You actually met most of them in the Start Now survey that (we hope) you completed earlier in this chapter. In the chapters to come, we explain which of these techniques are most effective as well as how to use them and for which subjects to use them.

> *Close to half of what predicts learning is how you approach studying.*

A LOOK INSIDE THE CLASSROOM

If you have checked to see which study strategies you used by completing the Start Now survey, you may wonder what strategies other students tend to use. You may also wonder whether the strategies really matter in terms of class performance. Let's take a look at a real-world classroom study designed to figure out what students use to study and how these strategies relate to class performance. If you skipped the survey, this is a good time to go back and complete it.

Brianna Bartoszewki, one of Regan's undergraduate students, conducted a great classroom study that included a measure of all 10 study techniques included in the Start Now survey (Bartoszewski & Gurung, 2015). In addition, Brianna and Regan had students rate the course lecture and professor to see how the different factors related to exam scores in comparison to the study techniques students often use. In fact, in the Start Now section you completed a portion of the actual survey Brianna and Regan used.

TABLE 1.1. Ten Learning Techniques From Cognitive Science

Technique	Description	Utility	Chapter of this book
Spaced practice (aka distributed practice)	Implementing a schedule of practice that spreads out study activities over time	High	4
Retrieval practice (aka practice testing)	Self-testing or taking practice tests over to-be-learned material	High	5
Interleaved practice	Mixing different kinds of problems/material within a single study session	Moderate	6
Self-explanation	Generating an explanation for why an explicitly stated fact or concept is true	Moderate	6
Worked examples	Studying detailed examples of how to solve a problem	Moderate	6
Highlighting/underlining	Marking potentially important portions of to-be-learned materials while reading	Low	7
Rereading	Restudying text material again after an initial reading	Low	7
Summarizing	Writing summaries (of various lengths) of to-be-learned texts	Low	7
Imagery	Attempting to form mental images of text materials while reading or listening	Low	7
Keyword mnemonic	Using keywords and mental imagery to associate verbal materials	Low	7

Note. Data from Dunlosky et al. (2013).

The students listed their favorite class and then answered questions about their own study habits in regard to this class. Figure 1.4 displays the extent to which each technique was used. Does it map what you use most? Not surprisingly, some techniques, such as rereading notes and memorizing key terms, appear high on the list, even though these techniques are not as effective as others.

However, the students in this study also used many techniques that we know work best and that we focus on in this book. For example, highly effective techniques, such as practice testing, were used often. The use of some techniques was also associated with the use of others. For example, students who used highlighting/underlining as a learning technique also used interleaved practice, keyword mnemonic, imagery for text, and rereading. Don't worry if some of these terms seem foreign to you; in later chapters we explain them in depth and provide plenty of examples.

The good news for you is that the results of this study suggest you should combine different ways of studying to improve academic performance. How do you do this? What are these different techniques sneak previewed in Table 1.1? To find out, you can jump ahead to Part II of this book.

HUDDLE UP

In American football, you often see the players quickly gather in a circle before a play. In this huddle, they summarize key strategies to attack the job at hand: to win the game. In keeping with our "study like a champion" theme, we end each chapter with a huddle of sorts in which we bring together key elements from the chapter designed to help you win the game. In this chapter, we have shared that students (and instructors) believe many myths about learning. The best way to find out what works is to do scientific research. Accordingly, when we discuss which strategies work best, we include a description of

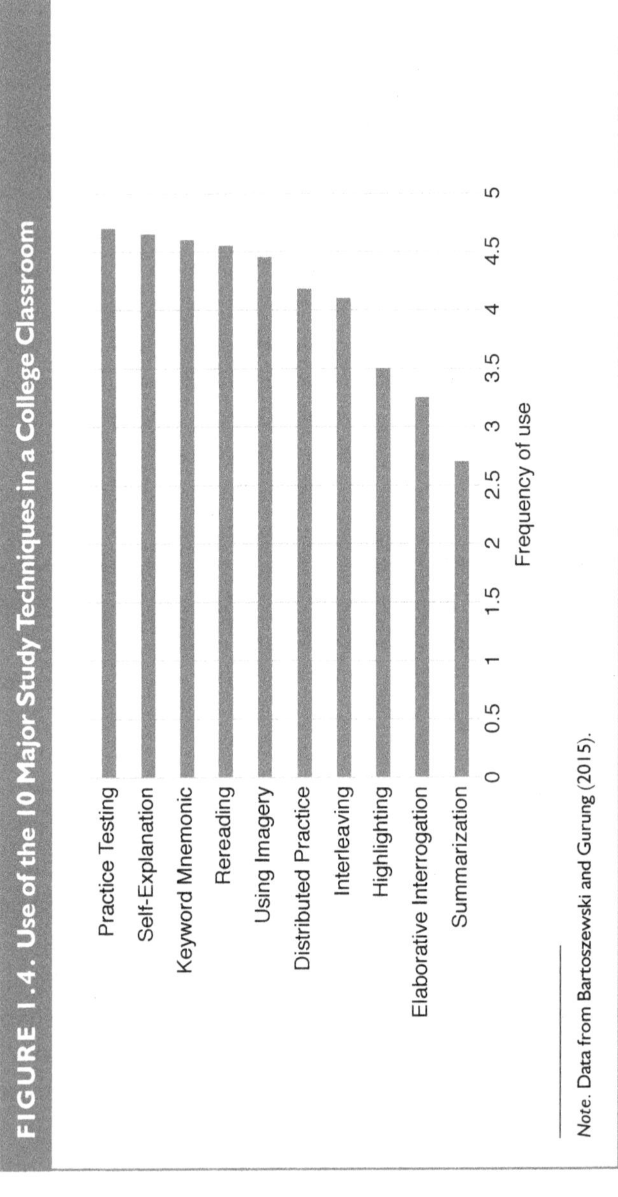

FIGURE 1.4. Use of the 10 Major Study Techniques in a College Classroom

Note. Data from Bartoszewski and Gurung (2015).

some of the scientific research—and, of course, we explain how to use the most effective strategies, so you can immediately make use of them to study like a champion.

Key Training Tips

- Study Champions do not believe the many myths surrounding learning and realize many factors influence learning. Do not fall prey to them.
- To borrow a phrase from the gymnastics world, Sticking Your Landing involves using only the most effective study techniques (not all 10).

Go for the Gold With an Advanced Reading

De Bruyckere, P., Kirschner, P. A., & Hulshof, C. D. (2015). *Urban myths about learning and education*. Elsevier.

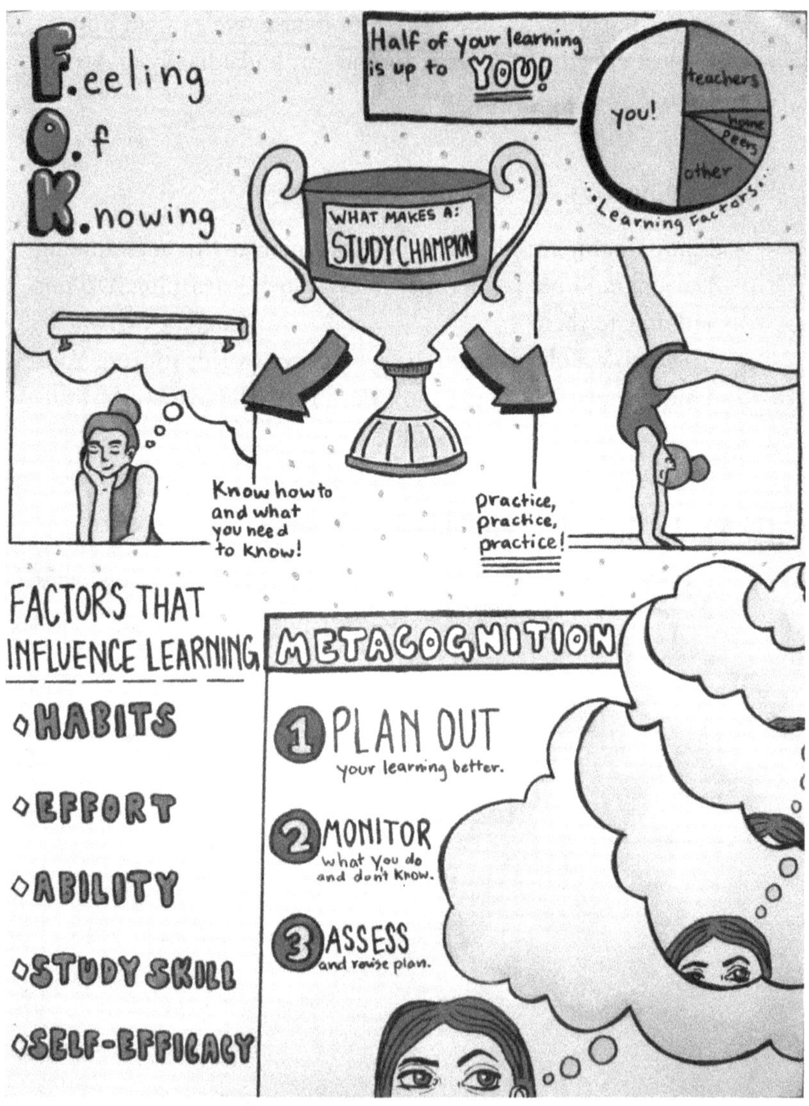

Drawing by Paige Herrboldt. Printed with permission.

CHAPTER 2

FIRST THINGS FIRST: PLANNING!

In this chapter, you will learn

- what your procrastination level is,
- how you can build your self-control, and
- some of the best ways to plan all your activities to make it likely that they get done.

In the 1960s, the city of Sydney, Australia, wanted to have something that would draw droves of people. City leaders invited architects from far and wide to submit plans for an eye-catching structure that the world had never seen. The winning bid was a building that would evoke a ship with multiple sails, billowing full of wind. You probably have seen pictures of the Sydney Opera House, but you may not know the story behind it. The building was planned to be completed in 4 years with a budget of $7,000,000. By the time the building was finished, the cost was $102,000,000, and it was 14 years later. Yes, more than $100,000,000 instead of $7,000,000—more than 14 times the original estimate! This clearly was an epic fail and is a key example of why planning is important.

Why was the project so delayed and overbudget? The city's plans did not account for all aspects of the process. The building was set in a harbor, which meant the foundation had to be built in water. The elaborate roof imposed significant structural demands on the materials used. The foundation kept sinking, and the costs for the right substance to withstand the stressors of the design drove the price up (Holliday, 2017). The city planners pictured the final product but not all the possible barriers to reaching that product.

Every academic week, thousands of students make similar planning mistakes. When we spoke to Daryl, one of our students, one Friday, he said he planned on writing two papers and reading for three other classes over the weekend. On Monday, he shared that he had forgotten that it was his partner's birthday and essentially spent all of Sunday celebrating. His car also broke down on Saturday, which affected his plans. To top it all off, as he was snacking and channel surfing Saturday night, he found a movie he really liked. Although he wanted to watch only until he finished eating, he ended up watching the whole thing (and eating more than he planned on, too). We all experience similar times in life when our plans do not work out for one reason or another.

One of the first essential elements of studying like a champion is to plan well. In this chapter, we discuss many elements that relate to good planning, ask you to test yourself on procrastination, and we provide some pragmatic tools that will help you plan well.

Start Now: Measure Your Procrastination Level

Instructions: A large number of studies have shown that procrastination, which is an actual, measurable personality trait, is generally linked to poor learning and negative outcomes. Don't be fooled by some social media posts that suggest that purposefully delaying tasks might be a beneficial strategy for some students. There is no evidence to support that idea (Pinxten et al., 2019). If you are a procrastinator, then you will need to pay even more attention to the planning strategies discussed in this chapter. Determine how much of a procrastinator you are by completing the following scale.

Your Instructions: People may use the following statements to describe themselves. For each statement, decide whether the statement is uncharacteristic or characteristic of you using the following 5-point scale. Note that the 3 on the scale is *Neutral*—the statement is neither characteristic nor uncharacteristic of you. In the box to the right of each statement, fill in the number on the 5-point scale that best describes you.

Extremely uncharacteristic	Moderately uncharacteristic	Neutral	Moderately characteristic	Extremely characteristic
1	2	3	4	5

1. I often find myself performing tasks that I had intended to do days before.	
2. I do not do assignments until just before they are to be handed in.	
3. When I am finished with a library book, I return it right away regardless of the date it is due.	
4. When it is time to get up in the morning, I most often get right out of bed.	
5. A letter may sit for days after I write it before mailing it.	
6. I generally return phone calls promptly.	
7. Even with jobs that require little else except sitting down and doing them, I find they seldom get done for days.	
8. I usually make decisions as soon as possible.	
9. I generally delay before starting on work I have to do.	
10. I usually have to rush to complete a task on time.	

(*continues*)

Extremely <u>un</u>characteristic	Moderately <u>un</u>characteristic	Neutral	Moderately characteristic	Extremely characteristic
1	2	3	4	5

11. When preparing to go out, I am seldom caught having to do something at the last minute.	
12. In preparing for some deadline, I often waste time by doing other things.	
13. I prefer to leave early for an appointment.	
14. I usually start an assignment shortly after it is assigned.	
15. I often have a task finished sooner than necessary.	
16. I always seem to end up shopping for birthday or Christmas gifts at the last minute.	
17. I usually buy even an essential item at the last minute.	
18. I usually accomplish all the things I plan to do in a day.	
19. I am continually saying, "I'll do it tomorrow."	
20. I usually take care of all the tasks I have to do before I settle down and relax for the evening.	

To get your procrastination score, first circle the following questions: 3, 4, 6, 8, 11, 13, 14, 15, 18, 20. For each of these questions, convert the number you listed to a new number using this simple formula. If you put down a 1, make it a 5; for a 2, make it a 4; for a 4, put down a 2; and for a 5, put down a 1. Now add together all your numbers. The resulting sum is your procrastination score.

The higher your score, the more of a procrastinator you are. Have a friend or classmate calculate their score and see how you compare.

Note. From "At Last, My Research Article on Procrastination," by C. Lay, 1986, *Journal of Research in Personality, 20*(4), pp. 474–495 (https://doi.org/10.1016/0092-6566(86)90127-3). Copyright 1986 by Elsevier. Reprinted with permission.

THE IMPORTANCE OF SELF-REGULATION

Do you have a good sense of yourself? We do not mean the big question, "Who am I?" (although we are sure that the question keeps some up at night). In the context of this book, we mean, "Are you good at setting goals for what you need to learn, do you develop plans to accomplish those goals, monitor your progress, and modify the plans when needed?" Doing all this means you are high in *self-regulation* (Hacker & Bol, 2019). Self-regulation is the key to studying like a champion.

The main idea of self-regulation is that there is a loop whereby you plan, monitor, and then evaluate your performance (see Figure 2.1). Cognitive scientists identify the three main phases of this loop: (a) the Forethought Phase, (b) the Performance Phase, and (c) the Self-Reflection Phase (Zimmerman, 2008). Your performance and your success result from how well you pay attention to specific elements in this loop. In the *Forethought Phase*, you break down what you want to study into subparts and set your goals for what you want to accomplish. How well you think you can accomplish the goal (self-efficacy), whether you expect to succeed (outcome expectation), your motivation to do it, and your interest all influence your goal setting and how successfully you move into the next phase.

The *Performance Phase* is where self-control plays a big part. Can you focus your attention? Can you limit distractions? Notice that the challenge here is to create the best conditions for you to study (or complete whatever task you have). The more effectively you set the stage for learning, the more likely it is to happen. A big

FIGURE 2.1. The Cycle of Self-Regulation

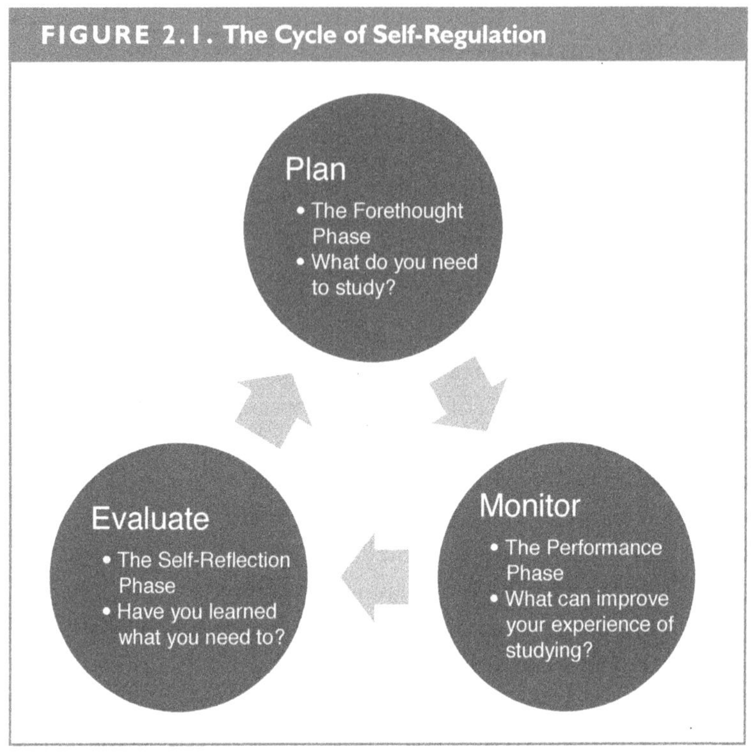
Plan
• The Forethought Phase
• What do you need to study?
Monitor
• The Performance Phase
• What can improve your experience of studying?
Evaluate
• The Self-Reflection Phase
• Have you learned what you need to?

part of the Performance Phase is paying attention to what you know and your experience of studying. If you feel you are not understanding a concept, or if you find the material boring, try doing something positive and constructive. Perhaps you can take a short, fast walk. Maybe you want to listen to a podcast on a topic you wanted to know more about. These two options are good ideas. You may also want to just pick up your phone and dive into social media, but that will not solve the problem. The key is to train yourself to recognize your progress, or lack thereof, and adapt to make progress more likely. This self-observation may involve recording your behavior, thoughts, and feelings or just being more mentally aware of them. This will help you plan and adjust better.

In the final stage, *Self-Reflection*, you establish a standard of performance and measure your performance in relation to that standard. For example, you could aim to study until you got at least 80% correct on a chapter quiz. Stop studying, take the quiz, and if your score is less than 80, go back and review the material again. Your own estimation, feelings, or subjective judgment of whether you have learned may not match an objective measure of learning, such as an exam score. In addition, your feeling of how much you know and how well an exam went may not match your exam score. This match is called *calibration*, and cognitive science has a good sense of the factors that influence your calibration (Hacker & Bol, 2019). Good self-regulators are also well calibrated, so developing both of these key cognitive components will help you better understand how to study like a champion.

A wide range of studies point to three main conclusions about calibration. First, most people are overconfident in how well they know material: Ironically, the lower your performance, the greater the overconfidence. David Dunning and Justin Kruger (1999) captured this effect in a phenomenon that now bears their names. They showed that calibration is particularly difficult for people with little knowledge of a topic who still, their lack of knowledge notwithstanding, believe they really know the material well even in the face of objective evidence to the contrary. The *Dunning–Kruger effect* seems to stem from the fact that if you do not have a minimal level of knowledge about a topic, your metacognitive abilities related to it are thwarted. Because people are often unaware of their minimal knowledge, they are oblivious they are being wrongly overconfident.

Second, our calibration errors are surprisingly resistant to change. To give one extreme example, even after 13 exams during a semester, students in an educational psychology course remained overconfident—they did not adjust their study habits (Foster et al., 2017). Our judgments are sometimes even more consistent than our performance. Finally, and unsurprisingly, our judgment of how much we know after an exam is better calibrated than judgments made before an exam. So, now you know about calibration, but what are you going to do about it?

The research on improving calibration—and, consequently, performance—has yielded a lot of mixed results, but we do have some tips for you. In two studies, the results showed that being well instructed, practicing the task at hand and material to be learned, being rewarded, and receiving good feedback were all related to increased exam scores from the first to a second exam (Callender et al., 2016). Note that control of only one of these—practice—lies in your own hands. If your instructor does not give you clear instructions, or if you feel you are not getting enough feedback on your work, then we urge you to ask. Asking for changes to teaching on the basis of the research is not a new idea, but most students do not think to do it (Putnam et al., 2016).

BUILDING YOUR SELF-REGULATION SKILLS

You may have heard about the marshmallow study. Psychologist Walter Mischel (2014) gave nearly 500 kids a choice. They had a really tasty-looking marshmallow put in front of them that they could eat whenever they wanted, or they could wait until a little longer and get two marshmallows instead. While the children were deciding, the researchers left the room. Some kids ate what was in front of them right away. Some delayed their gratification by waiting until the researchers returned—those children earned two marshmallows! This study is famous because Mischel found that the kids who could delay their gratification to obtain two marshmallows (or, in another version of the study, an extra Oreo cookie) did better in life. Yes, he followed those same children for years and discovered that the ones who delayed gratification were more successful.

Delay of gratification is one form of self-regulation and very relevant—often, we do not start studying (or keep away from work) early enough and instead turn to a more enjoyable, gratifying task, such as watching a movie, going out with friends, and so on. It is tough to wait for a reward until after the hard work has been done, but we encourage you to do so. Some easy ways to delay gratification are to set specific time or project milestones whereby you do not partake of the fun activity until a certain amount of time has passed (e.g., 30 minutes) or until you have completed a set amount of work (e.g., finished reading a chapter). Building self-regulation involves some clear-cut stages that greatly build on delay of gratification and directly map onto what you have to do as a student.

> *People who can delay gratification do better at planning, monitoring, and evaluating their learning.*

The key goals for you to build self-regulation are to *plan*, *monitor*, and *evaluate* your learning. Although these goals are easy to understand, doing them is tougher. To help you out, we provide some explicit questions for you to ask yourself. These questions, shown in Table 2.1 and modified from the work of Tanner (2012), are very clear-cut. For each class, ask yourself the questions listed in the table.

ASSESS YOUR METACOGNITION LEVEL

You may have an everyday sense of the concepts we are talking about (e.g., monitoring), but to truly study like a champion you also need a good sense of your metacognition skills. Thankfully, some great surveys can help you evaluate and develop your skills.

TABLE 2.1. Sample Self-Questions to Promote Student Metacognition About Learning

Activity	Planning	Monitoring	Evaluating
Class session	• What are the goals of the class session going to be? • What do I already know about this topic? • How could I best prepare for the class session? • Where should I sit, and what should I be doing (or not doing) to best support my learning during class? • What questions do I already have about this topic that I want to find out more about?	• What insights am I having as I experience this class session? What confusions? • What questions are arising for me during the class session? Am I writing them down somewhere? • Do I find this interesting? Why or why not? How could I make this material personally relevant? • Can I distinguish important information from details? If not, how will I figure this out?	• What was today's class session about? • What did I hear today that is in conflict with my prior understanding? • How did the ideas of today's class session relate to previous class sessions? • What do I need to actively do now to get my questions answered and my confusions clarified? • What did I find most interesting about class today?

Active-learning task and/or homework assignment	• What is the instructor's goal in having me do this task? • What are all the things I need to do to successfully accomplish this task? • What resources do I need to complete the task? How will I make sure I have them? • How much time do I need to complete the task? • If I have done something like this before, how could I do a better job this time?	• What strategies am I using that are working well or not working well to help me learn? • What other resources could I be using to complete this task? What action should I take to get these? • What is most challenging for me about this task? Most confusing? • What could I do differently mid-assignment to address these challenges and confusions?	• To what extent did I successfully accomplish the goals of the task? • To what extent did I use the resources available to me? • If I were the instructor, what would I identify as strengths of my work and flaws in my work? • When I do an assignment or task like this again, what do I want to remember to do differently? What worked well for me that I should do next time?

(*continues*)

TABLE 2.1. Sample Self-Questions to Promote Student Metacognition About Learning (*Continued*)

Quiz or exam	• What strategies will I use to study (e.g., study groups, problem sets, evaluating text figures, challenging myself with practice quizzes, and/or going to office hours and review sessions)? • How much time do I plan on studying? Over what period of time and for how long each time I sit down do I need to study? • Which aspects of the course material should I spend more or less time on, based on my current understanding?	• To what extent am I being systematic in my studying of all the material for the exam? • To what extent am I taking advantage of all the learning support available to me? • Am I struggling with my motivation to study? If so, do I remember why I am taking this course? • Which of my confusions have I clarified? How was I able to get them clarified? • Which confusions remain, and how am I going to get them clarified?	• What about my exam preparation worked well that I should remember to do next time? • What did not work so well that I should not do next time or that I should change? • What questions did I not answer correctly? Why? How did my answer compare with the suggested correct answer? • What confusions do I have that I still need to clarify?

Overall course	• Why is it important to learn the material in this course? • How does success in this course relate to my career goals? • How am I going to actively monitor my learning in this course? • What do I most want to learn in this course? • What do I want to be able to do by the end of this course?	• In what ways is the teaching of this course supportive of my learning? How could I maximize this? • In what ways is the teaching in this course not supportive of my learning? How could I compensate for or change this? • How interested am I in this course? How confident am I in my learning? What could I do to increase my interest and confidence?	• What will I still remember 5 years from now that I learned in this course? • What advice would I give a friend about how to learn the most in this course? • If I were to teach this course, how would I change it? • What have I learned about how I learn in this course that I could use in my future courses? In my career?

Note. Inspired by Ertmer and Newby (1996), Schraw (1998), and Coutinho (2007). Adapted from "Promoting Student Metacognition," by K. D. Tanner, 2012, *CBE–Life Sciences Education*, *11*(2), pp. 113–120. CC BY-NC.

The Metacognitive Awareness Inventory (Schraw & Dennison, 1994) is one of our favorites. Instead of showing you the entire scale as you would see it as a research participant, we will let you behind the curtain and show you the inventory broken down into the subparts it measures.

Read each statement in Figure 2.2 carefully. Consider whether the statement is true or false as it generally applies to you when you are in the role of a learner (student, attending classes, etc.). Determine whether each statement is true or false, giving yourself a 1 for "true" answers and a 0 when you answer "false." When you are finished, total up your score in each category.

WHAT'S THE EVIDENCE? A LOOK INSIDE THE CLASSROOM

What does the theoretical mumbo-jumbo in the survey look like in practice? Let us show you. A recent classroom-based study conducted by Hong and colleagues (2020) is one of the best examples of pulling together key measures in one study. Hong et al. ambitiously focused on many different elements of metacognition. Stand back and watch out: You will not only see some key applications and illustrations of what we talk about in this chapter but also some surprises. Here is what the researchers did. They homed in on a large introductory biology class and looked at the relationship between study behaviors and the exam scores of the 1,326 students who took it. The duration of the study was more than 2 years, something else you do not see a lot in this kind of research.

The study was comprehensive. First, students completed a survey at the start of each semester. Survey responses were then used to predict how much they learned, measured by using their exam scores. To make the study easier for the students, the survey was embedded in a learning management system (LMS). You probably also use an LMS, such as Canvas, D2L, or something similar.

FIGURE 2.2. Metacognitive Awareness Inventory Rating Guide

Metacognitive Awareness Inventory (MAI) Scoring Guide

Directions: For each *True* and *Rather True,* give yourself 1 point in the Score column. For each *False* and *Rather False*, give yourself 0 points in the score column. Total the score of each category and place in the box.

KNOWLEDGE ABOUT COGNITION

DECLARATIVE KNOWLEDGE

5. I understand my intellectual strengths and weaknesses.		
10. I know what kind of information is most important to learn.		
12. I am good at organizing information.		
16. I know what the teacher expects me to learn.		
17. I am good at remembering information.		
20. I have control over how well I learn.		
32. I am a good judge of how well I understand something.		
46. I learn more when I am interested in the topic.		
TOTAL		

PROCEDURAL KNOWLEDGE

3. I try to use strategies that have worked in the past.		
14. I have a specific purpose for each strategy I use.		
27. I am aware of what strategies I use when I study.		
33. I find myself using helpful learning strategies automatically.		
TOTAL		

CONDITIONAL KNOWLEDGE

15. I learn best when I know something about the topic.		
18. I use different learning strategies depending on the situation.		
26. I can motivate myself to learn when I need to.		
29. I use my intellectual strengths to compensate for my weaknesses.		
35. I know when each strategy I use will be most effective.		
TOTAL		

(*continues*)

FIGURE 2.2. Metacognitive Awareness Inventory Rating Guide (*Continued*)

REGULATION OF COGNITION

PLANNING

4. I pace myself while learning in order to have enough time.		
6. I think about what I really need to learn before I begin a task.		
8. I set specific goals before I begin a task.		
22. I ask myself questions about the material before i begin.		
23. I think of several ways to solve a problem and choose the best one.		
42. I read instructions carefully before I begin a task.		
45. I organize my time to best accomplish my goals.		
TOTAL		

INFORMATION MANAGEMENT STRATEGIES

9. I slow down when I encounter important information.		
13. I consciously focus my attention on important information.		
30. I focus on the meaning and significance of new information.		
31. I create my own examples to make information more meaningful.		
37. I draw pictures or diagrams to help me understand while learning.		
39. I try to translate new information into my own words.		
41. I use the organizational structure of the text to help me learn.		
43. I ask myself if what I'm reading is related to what I already know.		
47. I try to break studying down into smaller steps.		
48. I focus on overall meaning rather than specifics.		
TOTAL		

COMPREHENSION MONITORING

1. I ask myself periodically if I am meeting my goals.		
2. I consider several alternatives to a problem before I answer.		
11. I ask myself if I have considered all options when solving a problem.		

FIGURE 2.2. Metacognitive Awareness Inventory Rating Guide (*Continued*)

21. I periodically review to help me understand important relationships.		
28. I find myself analyzing the usefulness of strategies while I study.		
34. I find myself pausing regularly to check my comprehension.		
49. I ask myself questions about how well I am doing while learning something new.		
TOTAL		

DEBUGGING STRATEGIES

25. I ask others for help when I don't understand something.		
40. I change strategies when I fail to understand.		
44. I reevaluate my assumptions when I get confused.		
51. I stop and go back over new information that is not clear.		
52. I stop and reread when I get confused.		
TOTAL		

EVALUATION

7. I know how well I did once I finish a test.		
19. I ask myself if there was an easier way to do things after I finish a task.		
24. I summarize what I've learned after I finish.		
36. I ask myself how well I accomplish my goals once I´m finished.		
38. I ask myself if I have considered all options after I solve a problem.		
49. I ask myself if I learned as much as I could have once I finish a task.		
TOTAL		

Note. From "Assessing Metacognitive Awareness," by G. Schraw and R. S. Dennison, 1994, *Contemporary Educational Psychology*, *19*(4), pp. 473–475 (https://doi.org/10.1006/ceps.1994.1033). Copyright 1994 by Elsevier. Reprinted with permission.

In addition to the main measures of interest, the survey also captured demographic information, such as age, ethnicity, and year in school. Also included were psychological measures of motivation, such as self-efficacy, achievement goals, task value, and cost. There were four exams in the class, and all were completed on paper. The exams were a combination of multiple-choice questions and short essays.

Given what we have talked about so far regarding metacognition, you should be wondering about how Hong et al. (2020) measured it. This is where the study seems to go undercover. Like something out of a James Bond movie, the students' learning behaviors were captured in a very subtle way. The researchers measured metacognitive processes by analyzing how and when students looked at the syllabi and study guides on the LMS. Guess what? Syllabi and study guides can be extremely useful for planning your studying. Both these types of aids can help you direct your attention to what is important to learn. Good syllabi and study guides also specify the level of understanding needed for the content tested on an exam. Something some students may not know is that everything they do on their online course sites can be examined. Instructors can tell when you looked at a page, how long you looked at it, when you took a quiz, and a whole host of other factors (Gurung, 2020).

In this study, Hong et al. (2020) accessed the LMS data showing the extent to which students interacted with the digital resources on the course site and the students' exam scores. Aside from accessing the syllabi and study guides, students in the study had the opportunity to monitor their learning by completing ungraded self-assessment quizzes. These no-stakes assessments allowed students to rehearse their knowledge and obtain feedback about how accurate the assessments were when they took the tests (important study strategies that we discuss in detail in Chapter 6). In addition, students could check their grades to monitor performance as well (i.e., clicking on a My Grades site to view current points earned).

In short, the LMS traced which monitoring tools the students used and captured the frequency with which students accessed those tools. Also, notice that tools to help you monitor the key components of self-regulation discussed above—planning, monitoring, assessing—are all available to you in your LMS.

By now, you probably want to know the results. Although this summary gives you only the highlights, the entire article makes for stimulating reading, especially in regard to the link between motivation and metacognition. We are going to focus on the results related to planning and monitoring. The data show that there were two main groups of students in the class, as suggested by their behavioral profiles. One group practiced self-assessment only through repeated monitoring of their performance on ungraded quizzes (Hong et al., 2020). These quizzes were designed for students to judge whether they knew the content. What is curious about this set of students is that they focused on self-assessment quizzes alone, typically not engaging in other available metacognitive processes or accessing other available tools.

The second group of students had a different behavioral profile: They engaged only in planning, using exam resources, and checking of grades, with nearly zero self-assessment on quizzes. This second group had better exam scores. Those with low scores typically engaged in little metacognitive processing, which nicely supports our advice.

> *Students who refer to their online syllabi and study guides to plan or monitor their learning perform better on exams than students who do not use these resources.*

Finally, the investigation revealed an important warning. Most students did not take advantage of the resources on their LMS. In fact, 75% of students in the study did not fully tap into exactly the items designed to aid their metacognition. Do not make the same mistake. Use what is available to you when you plan, monitor, and evaluate your learning.

IN PRACTICE: SOME RECOMMENDATIONS FOR PLANNING

It is always easier to start afresh. Sometimes we want a do-over and a chance to not repeat the mistakes of the past. A new school year, or even a new semester or term, provides just such a chance to correct what you did not like. Similar to the gusto with which people face the new year, making New Year's resolutions, you can celebrate the start of a new academic year as a chance to rectify past studying mistakes. This chance is even bigger during transitions. The move from high school to college is a big milestone. The move from your first year to your second, second to third, and third to senior year each provide clear-cut points to change behaviors.

The biggest mistake made when we try to plan is that we do not always include everything in the plan. The problem here is that we often fail to include both fun activities and healthy activities (and separating these, acknowledging not everything fun is healthy) in our plans. We all like to have fun and often end up wanting to and doing so regardless of our plans. If not planned for, these extra activities can disrupt the studying plan. Both John and Regan have spoken to umpteen first-year students who, in celebrating their move to college, often revel in having few limitations and boundaries. By senior year, these students regret their wild and wanton early college years, when a lack of careful planning of their social activities threw a wrench in their academic plans.

Whether it is completing homework assignments or life's necessities, when we consciously and actively plan out what we have to do, the chances of getting all of our tasks done increase. To emphasize:

Planning well is one of the most important skills a person can develop. There are many benefits to thorough, intentional planning. Not only does good planning increase our likelihood of success and of getting the job done, it also can decrease the stress we experience. Accordingly, we hope you will use the tips in this chapter to help you plan better.

In the next few paragraphs, we discuss some basic steps.

First, you need to be aware of all the tasks you have to do. Most students are taking multiple classes. Make sure you have a clear sense of your weekly requirements. Pay attention to exactly how much you have to read, what you have to write, and when each assignment is due. Review each syllabus. Go to the page that lists when assignments are due, and enter each assignment, exam, and quiz in your calendar, planner, or to-do list right away. Use a tool—perhaps a calendar, planner, or app—to jot down everything so all your assignments are visible. Numerous planning apps are available that are calendar based or checklist based. You may want to check out Fantastical (https://flexibits.com/fantastical), Todoist (https://todoist.com/home), Microsoft To Do (https://todo.microsoft.com/tasks/), or similar apps. You may prefer using a paper planner or take this opportunity to get a fun calendar (The Office? Superheroes? Cute cats?). Pick something you will use! You may use more than one.

Then, enter it all in; write it all down. Color code the information by class or type of assignment. Also, for each class, set aside multiple times each week that you will work on the course (this helps you space your practice; see Chapter 4). You may consider having one large block of study time broken into segments when you will study for different classes.

Next, schedule time for other key activities, such as eating, sleep, and physical activity. Put in when you should go to bed and when you should wake up. This may prevent a Netflix binge or internet surfing session from extending too far into the night. Sleep is perhaps the single biggest health behavior that college students do not pay enough attention to. Getting more sleep is probably the single biggest factor that can increase your mood and productivity. If you schedule it, it is more likely to happen.

Now for something you have probably rarely heard: We suggest you go ahead and also include your fun activities in your plan. You need fun. We all need fun. Do not pretend like it does not exist. By adding it to your plan, you are being more realistic about how much time you have for your academic responsibilities. In our college days, both John and Regan often had great plans for the weekend in terms of all the work we thought we would get done. We rarely, if ever, thought of the parties, intramural sports, movies, and other fun things we wanted to do. It's no surprise that we did not get as much work done as we wanted. Now we know better and have the research experience to know that planning it all is better. If you do not factor in your social life you may well derail your work and study schedules.

Explicitly factoring in nonacademic activities has another benefit: You build in breaks that can actually reduce burnout and increase your productivity. This is particularly important for college students, who can find themselves in trouble if they get carried away with studying; planning in your social life acts as a safety valve (Gurung, 2014). When you plan, you consciously and explicitly acknowledge what you will allow yourself to do (e.g., stay up with pals until 1:00 a.m. every now and then) and what you will not (e.g., illegal, unsafe activities).

An example of a work week for someone with five classes is shown in Figure 2.3. Note the interweaving of study for different classes, the time scheduled for exercise, some flexible unscheduled time, time for fun, and time for meals. Even time to work on homework is specifically listed. You should plan on doing work on every

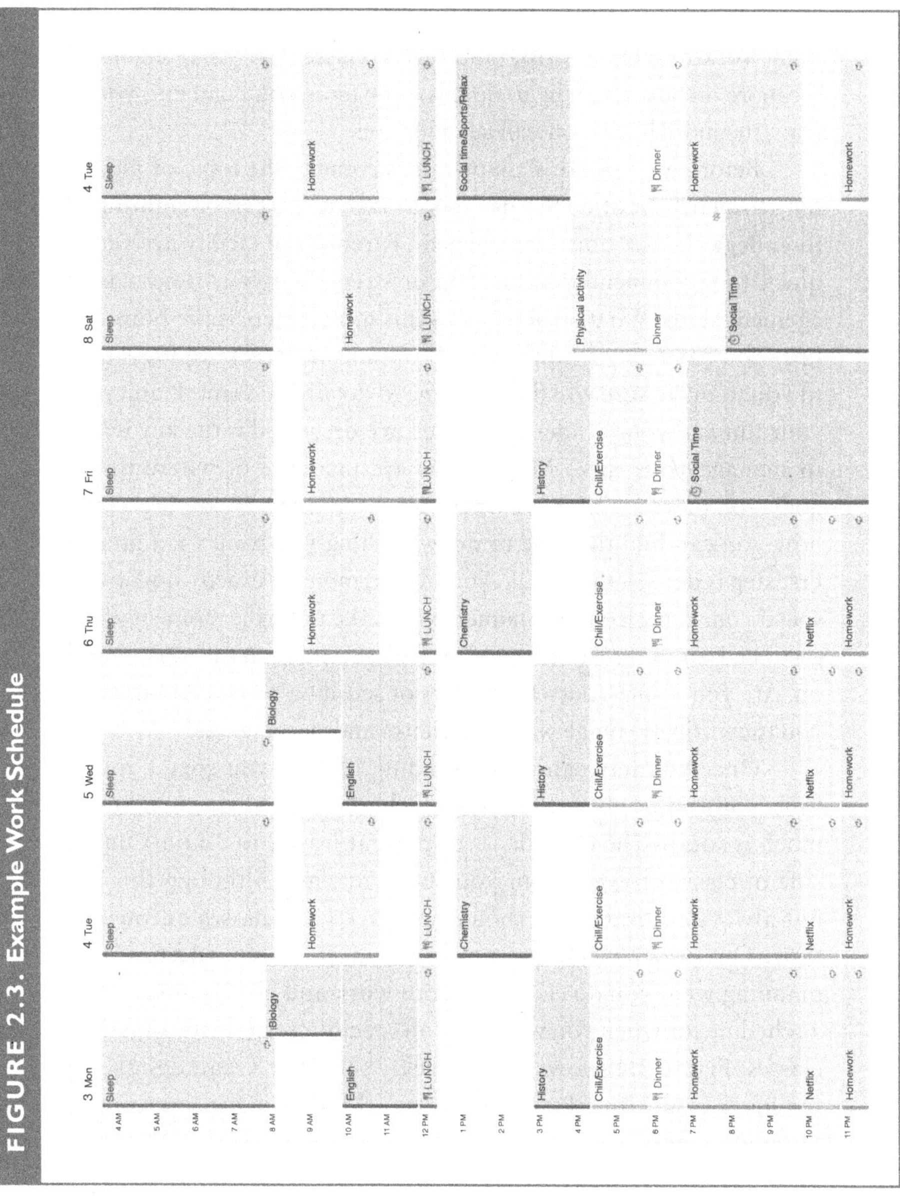

FIGURE 2.3. Example Work Schedule

class at least two to three times a week; break up each big block of homework to include work on different classes (see Chapters 4–6 for more on how and why to do this). The more you build into your plan, the more likely you will get a lot done.

Before we close this chapter, let's connect the topic of planning to a concept often discussed in University 101 or orientation-to-college classes: time management. Parents and faculty are very quick to recommend you develop or strengthen your time management skills. What, exactly, does this mean? Here is the bottom line: You have only a finite amount of time in a week, and it is up to you to make sure you find the time to do all you want. Planning your fun and your academics as we have described is the key way to manage your time. Many of us are unaware of where time goes—or, more specifically, where we waste time. If you are sure how you can find the time to do everything you want to, a good first step is doing a time audit. For 1 week, monitor exactly how you spend your time, from the moment you wake up to the moment you go to bed. At the end of the week, see what you spent the most time on. Are you losing yourself in hours of scrolling social media? Are you (unwittingly) binge watching shows and sleeping less?

Once you have an understanding of how you spend your time, you will be able to see how much of it is academic and how much is social. The old rule is to spend at least 2 to 3 hours outside of class for every hour you spend in class. Although this is not always accurate, you should still give your classes adequate time. One way to help your time management, in addition to planning what you do each day (both work and play), is to create a schedule for when you will work on specific components of your classes. Figure 2.4 shows you a weekly schedule Regan designed for his Introductory Psychology class. Modify it for your own different classes.

FIGURE 2.4. A Weekly Schedule Regan Designed for His Introductory Psychology Class

Sample Weekly Timeline - Intro. Psych

Tuesday

Work on your **other** classes so you **SPACE** out your work on Intro Psych.

Thursday

Work on other classes so you space out your work.

Weekend

Enjoy the outdoors. Get physical activity, spend time with friends and family.
Skim study plan for week ahead and polish Applied Learning Essay.
Take quiz (second and final time).

Monday

Take **pretest.**
Attend class.
Go over study plan: Match with notes, identify terms you are not understanding.
Finalize and submit your Applied Learning Essay.

Wednesday

Attend class.
Review **study plan** in the hour before class.
Look over notes from last class.
List **questions** for Dr. G (ask during or after class). Take 5 minutes after class to look over notes.
Take quiz (first attempt) after reviewing.

Friday

Review study plan and notes from week.
Look at the Applied Learning Essay due Monday, and **get started.**
Clarify instructions if needed.

HUDDLE UP

Regan remembers one of his graduate school advisor's favorite tricks to help him get more work done. His advisor asked all the students in the research lab to clearly state what their plans were for the term ahead. Regan found that the more explicitly he and his fellow students expressed their plans, the more productive and successful they all were. We often do not give planning as much thought as we should; making plans that are as detailed as possible increases the chances we will succeed in getting everything accomplished. Your classes will vary in terms of how much you have to read, how many assignments you have, and the types of exams you will have to take. Regardless of whether you are studying for an essay or multiple-choice exam, have to write a paper, or create a presentation, you need to have the time to do it. Even before you get to the specific cognitive strategies we discuss in Part II of this book, you must create the time to make sure you can accomplish all of your tasks.

Before going on to the next chapter, pick a class you find challenging, and plan your next week to give yourself more time with it. If you are reading this before the start of a term, that's even better. Even if you are picking this up midway into your semester, you can still turn things around. Make tomorrow a better planned day. Make next week more productive by planning how you will study or complete projects for each of your courses. Take the time you have left until the end of term to ramp up your planning game. Plan wisely to get the most out of your time in college. The rest of your life will be better for it.

Key Training Tips

- Study Champions develop a strong plan for when, what, and how they will study.

- Sticking Your Landing involves finding the best way to plan out a week, taking into account all your classwork and other responsibilities, and including time for friends and physical activity leads to success.

Go for the Gold With an Advanced Reading

Hong, W., Bernacki, M. L., & Perera, H. N. (2020). A latent profile analysis of undergraduates' achievement motivations and metacognitive behaviors, and their relations to achievement in science. *Journal of Educational Psychology, 112*(7), 1409–143. https://doi.org/10.1037/edu0000445

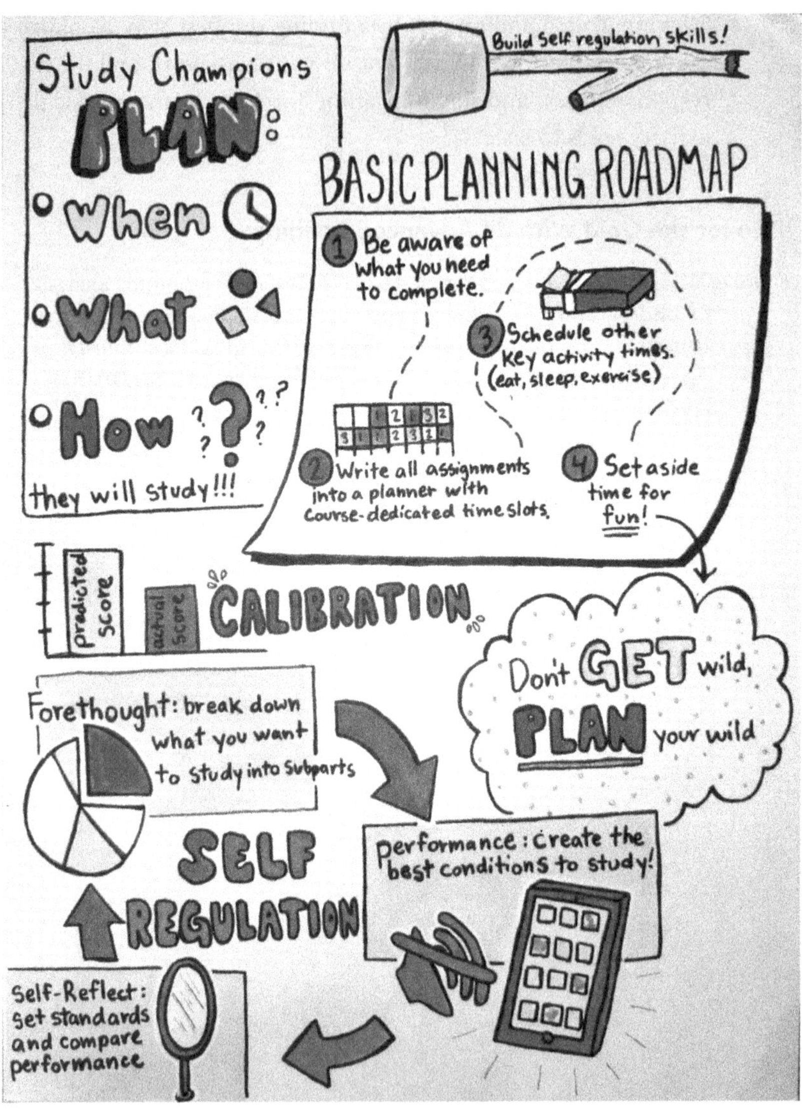

Drawing by Paige Herrboldt. Printed with permission.

CHAPTER 3

TAKE NOTES WELL

In this chapter, you will learn

- the best ways to take notes,
- the different purposes notes can take, and
- what you should DO with your notes (and when).

Imagine you are going to court to sue a drunk driver for damages. Your car was totaled, and it was no fault of yours at all. The driver had been at a party and clearly had much too much to drink. At the trial, you and your lawyer explain the details of what happened that day. As you turn your attention to the 12 jurors listening to your case, you notice something that disturbs you. None of the jurors are taking notes. They seem to be listening, but it's hard to be sure. Should you be concerned? Will not taking notes influence how much attention they pay to the case? Will the lapse affect their memory regarding the details and maybe even influence their deliberations and decision? Yes, yes, and yes.

As instructors, we often see students not taking any notes. Sometimes the student is just listening. More often, the student is texting or surfing the internet on their laptop. Even note-takers sometimes text and surf the internet (two activities not allowed for jurors), resulting in poorer quality notes. One of the first things we do when we talk with students who performed poorly on an exam is look at how they take notes. After all, another essential element of studying like a champion is to take notes and take them well so that you can focus on all the essential concepts of a particular class while you study. In this chapter, we discuss the main functions served by note-taking, have you test your own note-taking, and provide some explicit ways to take good notes.

In Chapter 2, we discussed self-regulation, and note-taking is a key example of self-regulation in that you have to decide when something is important enough to write down, check whether you have captured it correctly, and review by testing yourself on the notes. Do not be tempted to skip this chapter if you already take notes. As you shall soon see, it is not just the act of taking notes, but the quality of the notes you take, that matters. To begin, let's look at the level of your note-taking skills. Figure 3.1 provides a road map

FIGURE 3.1. Notes on the Note-Taking Chapter

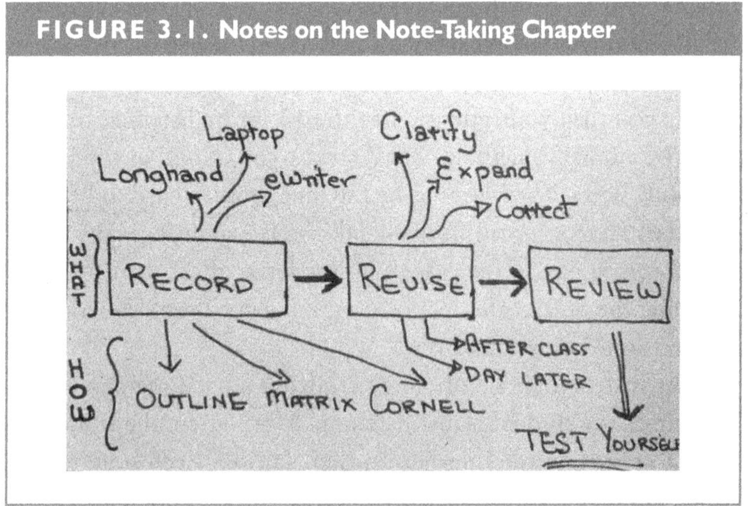

for the key processes in note-taking and gives you a big-picture view of what to expect in this chapter.

Start Now: How Are Your Note-Taking Skills?

The following set of questions was designed to measure the quality of your note-taking. Think about one specific class you have right now. To what extent does the way you take notes comply with the descriptions given? After you read all the questions and list a value, reflect on your answers as you read the rest of the chapter.

Use the following scale: 1 = *Strongly Disagree*, 2 = *Disagree*, 3 = *Neither Agree nor Disagree*, 4 = *Agree*, 5 = *Strongly Agree*.

Section I

1. _____ I write down whatever I hear the lecturer say.
2. _____ I make a verbatim record of all course content that the lecturer wrote.
3. _____ I write down the course content explained, even though I am already familiar with it.
4. _____ I write down anything the lecturer writes that is related to the course content.
5. _____ I try to write down all the points highlighted. In addition to writing down the concepts, I also write down the examples provided.

Section II

1. _____ I selectively write down the more important parts of the lecture content.
2. _____ I record lecture notes by summarizing the main points.
3. _____ I mark/highlight particularly important places in my notes.
4. _____ I refer to the content of the lecture handouts or textbooks and then select the information that must be recorded.

Section III

1. _____ When listening to a lecture, I think about related information or questions before writing notes down.
2. _____ I add homophones or examples that I think of in my notes to help me remember the contents of the lecture.
3. _____ In addition to the contents explained by the lecturer, I also write down my own opinions and ideas.

Section IV

1. _____ I use the outline method to make lecture notes.
2. _____ I use numbers to denote the order of the main topics.
3. _____ I use blank spaces to organize the main points of the content I have recorded.
4. _____ I use the outline of lecture handouts or textbooks to structure and organize the notes that I wrote.

Section V

1. _____ If there are sections of the lecture that I did not record in time, I immediately fill in the blanks by referring to a classmate's notes.
2. _____ I distinguish between the important and less important contents of the notes I wrote down.
3. _____ I check my notes to ensure that I did not miss any important content.
4. _____ I leave blank spaces in my notes so that I can supplement the contents in the future.
5. _____ If there is anything in my notes that I do not understand, I make marks/highlight it during the lecture.
6. _____ If there is anything that I do not understand during the lecture, I immediately refer to the contents of the textbook and then write them in my notes.

Add up your scores in each section. The key to success is to score as high as possible on this scale. So, how did you do? Was your score higher in some sections than others? Here is what the different sections measure: Section I measures Copying, Section II measures Key Point Selection, Section III measures Elaboration, Section IV measures Organization, and Section V measures Comprehension Monitoring. In the pages that follow, we unpack the rationale for why you should try to modify your note-taking to get a maximum score in each section.

Note. From "In-Class and After-Class Lecture Note-Taking Strategies," by P.-H. Chen, 2021, *Active Learning in Higher Education*, 22(3), pp. 245–260 (https://doi.org/10.1177/1469787419893490). Copyright 2021 by SAGE. Reprinted with permission.

FOCUS ON THE "HOW"

Look around your college classroom. How many students are taking notes? Research shows that over 95% of students report taking notes during a lecture (Morehead, Dunlosky, et al., 2019). Your classmates may have a notebook or a laptop in front of them, and when the professor speaks they seem to correspondingly write in their notebooks or type on their keyboards. Of course, you do not know what they are doing. They could be doodling, sketching, making a shopping list, or shopping online for hamster jackets. The fact is they are doing a lot of these things. Even if they were "only" taking notes, know that people take notes in many different ways.

> *The quality of your notes significantly influences how much you learn.*

At the core of it, note-taking seems easy: Open a notebook and start writing when the professor puts up a slide with words on it—maybe even write down as much as you can about what the professor says. If this is how you have been taking notes, get ready to consider some changes to improve the quality of your notes. After all, studies have found that the quality of your notes significantly influences how much you learn (e.g., Peverly & Wolf, 2019). Let's look at different approaches you may use to take notes and then review some other techniques you can try.

LAPTOP OR LONGHAND?

Let's tackle a key question right away: Should you use a computer to take notes or write them out longhand with a pen or pencil and paper? To help you understand the subtle answer to this question, we first need to introduce a key distinction in research about note-taking: its encoding and storage functions. These are fancy terms for otherwise-simple functions of note-taking. The *encoding function* pertains to the degree that actually taking notes—versus just listening to a lecture—will improve your understanding of or memory for that lecture, that is, how much note-taking helps you encode the information in the lecture. The *storage function* pertains to the degree to which studying those notes will improve your performance on exams, that is, how much you can store in memory about the lecture when you revise your notes and study them after taking them. The debate concerning whether to use laptops or longhand largely refers to the encoding function of note-taking: Will one method help you learn more while taking notes?

Some college professors ban the use of laptops in class, and you would be justified in assuming this is because research suggests that using laptops to take notes is not a good idea. In fact, a very popular study conducted some years ago, which was picked up by social media, bandied about by the press, and brandished by many faculty, suggested that indeed the pen is mightier than the laptop (Mueller & Oppenheimer, 2014). More recently, Morehead, Dunlosky, and Rawson (2019), as well as Urry and colleagues (2021), also compared longhand and laptop note-taking. The results they found were surprising, so let's take a closer look.

Morehead, Dunlosky, and Rawson (2019, Experiment 2) conducted a direct replication of Mueller and Oppenheimer's (2014) research by comparing different forms of note-taking and extended their research; specifically, college students were randomly assigned to one of four note-taking groups. One group took notes with pencil and paper (i.e., by longhand), and one group took notes on a laptop; these groups comprised the *direct replication*. For the extension of the prior research, another group took notes on an ewriter (a device with which the students wrote longhand on electronic paper), and a final group simply listened to the lectures (i.e., no–note-taking group). The lectures were two short TED Talks videos. After taking notes (or just listening), students immediately took a test on the content of the lectures; the test included questions that tapped students' memory for factual information (*factual knowledge*) from the lectures and questions that tapped how well they understood the concepts (*conceptual knowledge*). A week later, the groups who took notes returned to the laboratory to restudy the notes they had taken; they studied the notes for 7 minutes and then took another test on the material.

What did the researchers find? Figure 3.2 presents data from the immediate test, which measured the impact of these note-taking methods on the encoding function of note-taking. Several outcomes are notable. First, the scores of students who took notes by longhand (either on paper or the ewriter) versus those who used a laptop did not differ. This was true for both factual and conceptual questions. This outcome—that is, no difference between longhand and laptop note-taking—was also reported in another large-scale replication (Urry et al., 2021). Second, none of the groups who took notes outperformed the students who merely listened to the lecture! In other words, note-taking in this investigation had no impact on encoding. This outcome is relatively common, and even when taking notes has

FIGURE 3.2. Note-Taking Method

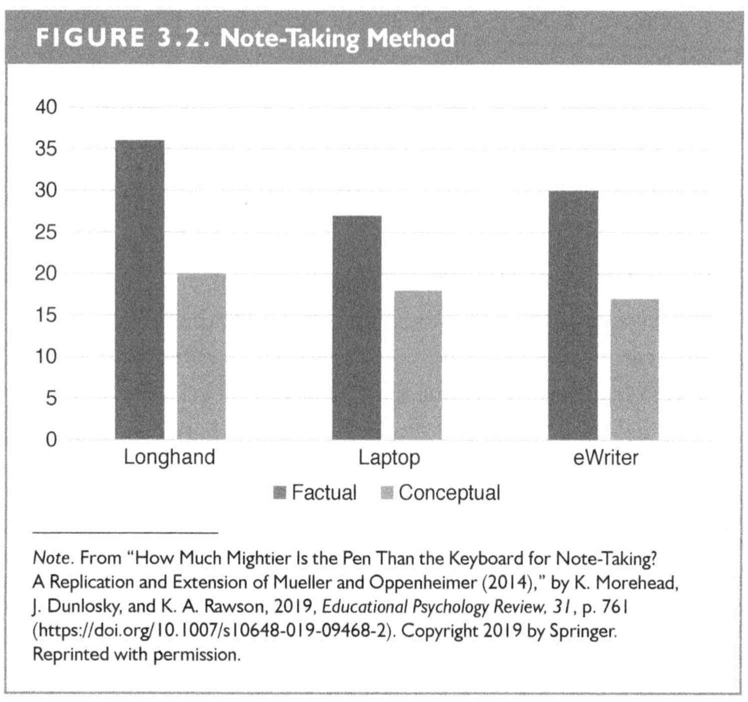

Note. From "How Much Mightier Is the Pen Than the Keyboard for Note-Taking? A Replication and Extension of Mueller and Oppenheimer (2014)," by K. Morehead, J. Dunlosky, and K. A. Rawson, 2019, *Educational Psychology Review, 31*, p. 761 (https://doi.org/10.1007/s10648-019-09468-2). Copyright 2019 by Springer. Reprinted with permission.

been found to boost students' encoding of a lecture, its impact has been minor. You will learn little extra by simply *taking* notes per se (whether you do so with a computer or by longhand), and certainly the simple act of taking notes will not lift you to the level of understanding required to excel on many class exams.

Finally, even when students restudied their notes a week later and took the delayed test, their performance on this test did not differ among the note-taking groups. In fact, the students did not appear to learn that much from restudying their notes; that is, notes did not appear to support the storage function of note-taking, either. In this case, however, one major limitation was that students were given only 7 minutes to study their notes; that is not enough time to use the most effective study strategies (which we discuss in Part II of the book). Most important, on the basis of these results, the story so far is that no one method of note-taking is superior for learning than another.

> *Between note-taking on a computer and note-taking by pen and paper, there is no clear winner.*

Some faculty may not like to hear this, but there is no clear note-taking winner. Nevertheless, another reason why professors may ban laptops is that computers can be distracting. In one investigation in which the researchers observed students using laptops in classrooms, the students spent only 37% of the time on class-related work (Ragan et al., 2014). The rest of the time, students were on social media sites or surfing the web. If a student was using the computer only to take notes, then the association of note-taking with learning and retention of material would be higher. So, if you think you can use the laptop exclusively for note-taking while in class, keep distraction at bay, and take notes well, the risks for laptop use are minimal. In some situations, a laptop may even be more beneficial than other note-taking methods. Most individuals can type faster than they write, which can help in classes where a professor talks quickly or when you need to copy the material verbatim. If instead the professor uses a lot of diagrams and figures, using longhand and paper would allow you to draw out associations. So, choose your note-taking method on the basis of the demands of the class and, of course, on your own comfort using one or the other to take quality notes!

Of course, on the basis of the results we have just described, you may be thinking that taking notes doesn't matter at all. Sure, the act of taking notes itself may not help you learn difficult course content, so what really matters is *having complete notes* so that you have access to the critical information you need to learn while studying for your course exams. Put differently, you should take high-quality notes, so as you consider which note-taking method to use it may help to take a step back and look at some different stages in the process of taking good notes. Doing so may help you understand how to become a better note-taker.

NOTES PLAY DIFFERENT ROLES

Notes are a resource to help you prepare for exams; as we have emphasized, they exist to help you with the storage function, to later learn the course content while preparing for exams. You still have to decide what is important in a lecture and when to write something down. For example, should you write down the story your instructor just told? Both of us like to tell stories when we teach, as do many instructors. The stories are not meant to be time-wasting tangents but to illustrate a concept or theory being discussed or an application of the material to life. When telling these stories, it appears that many students stop writing to listen, missing an opportunity to record what could serve as an important learning aid. This is an example that illustrates a key point of a lecture.

The role of note-taking may make more sense when you go behind the scenes to an *information-processing* theory of memory. To process information well, consider relying on a few cognitive strategies while taking notes (or studying them afterward). Later in this book, we discuss how to implement several of these strategies in detail, so for now this is just a brief preview of categories of strategies that are relevant to your note-taking:

- *rehearsal strategies*, whereby you retrieve information from memory;
- *elaboration strategies*, whereby you connect what you hear to what you know;
- *organization strategies*, whereby you connect new material into a cohesive structure;

- *metacognitive strategies*, which are similar to planning and monitoring (described in Chapter 2 and in Part II of this book); and
- *affective/motivational strategies*, which relate to attention, stress management, and time management.

Good note-taking should make your attention more selective, force you to organize your ideas, and relate the material to what you know; these are all critical elements of helping you learn. But let us be explicit here: Many of the processes listed above that lead to good learning are ones that you should also use when you later go back to revise and study your notes. Thus, what ultimately matters is taking complete, high-quality notes (Chen, 2021). Most often, simply copying down what the professor says or shows on the screen will not provide all the potential benefits of note-taking, although if you can get it all down, then no doubt you will have access to what the instructor wants you to know. With that said, having *a lot* of notes is not necessarily as important as having *the right* notes and subsequently studying them in the most effective ways (for details on how to study effectively, see Part II). With respect to note-taking quality, one investigation showed that college students captured only 11% of a lecture's critical ideas (Raver & Maydose, 2010), and another investigation revealed that students who missed taking down key ideas had only a 5% chance of remembering those ideas on an exam (Einstein et al., 1985).

WHAT VARIABLES PREDICT WHO TAKES BETTER NOTES?

Just as personality varies from person to person, such as with introverts and extroverts, so too can people be divided into major categories when it comes to note-taking. In fact, people's note-taking differs in some key ways, and consequently some variables predict who will take better notes. If you know the more effective characteristics of note-takers, you can use that information to improve your note-taking skills.

A small group of variables predict quality note-taking (see Peverly & Wolf, 2019, for a review). For instance, people who write faster tend to take better longhand notes, simply because they can get more complete notes. If you can keep your focus, rather than being distracted easily, you will take better notes. Students with higher verbal ability also take better notes. We realize that it may be difficult to change these variables quickly enough to take better notes tomorrow—after all, how could you speed up your writing (without taking a class on writing in shorthand), and your verbal ability has been formed across years of reading and interacting with language, so improving it in a flash will be tough. Even so, if you are using a laptop to take notes, turning off access to the internet is likely to reduce distractions and improve your note-taking. Another variable that you can control—how well you are prepared for a class lecture—promises to improve your skills.

You may wonder if your note-taking ability gets better the further along in college you are. Although we have not seen any studies that tested this in a longitudinal fashion, there is some evidence that what students do with notes varies with year in college. For example, Chen (2021) showed that students' after-class note strategies did vary among first-, second-, third-, and fourth-year students, as shown in Figure 3.3. As we discussed in the preceding section, the extent to which notes were used for elaboration, organization, and help-seeking were different across years, with more elaboration and organization taking place the first 2 years.

> *Completing the assigned reading before class helps you take better notes.*

One important factor in particular that relates to the quality of notes is background knowledge on a topic: Students who know more about a topic take more concise notes on that topic. So, do you rarely

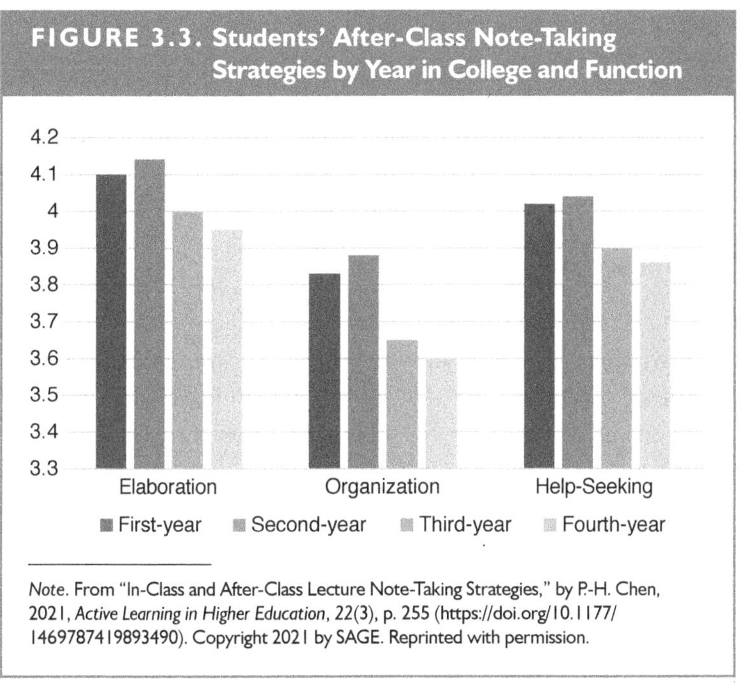

FIGURE 3.3. Students' After-Class Note-Taking Strategies by Year in College and Function

Note. From "In-Class and After-Class Lecture Note-Taking Strategies," by P.-H. Chen, 2021, *Active Learning in Higher Education*, 22(3), p. 255 (https://doi.org/10.1177/1469787419893490). Copyright 2021 by SAGE. Reprinted with permission.

read the assigned reading before going to class? If you don't, your note-taking may benefit from doing it. An assigned reading will include many of the terms or theories the instructor uses in the lecture, so reading it before a lecture will help you become a bit more familiar with it. Also, this familiarity may increase your note-taking speed because you will recognize what would otherwise be new, alien words, helping you also be more accurate and have more complete notes.

A PROCESS FOR USING NOTES: THE R3 METHOD

Record, Revise, Review: These steps make up the R3 method, which is hard to attribute to a single author but is a usable amalgam of many cognitive science research results. The R3 method helps you better organize your notes and the way you use your notes to learn. The first step focuses on getting as complete a set of notes as possible, whereas the next two steps involve subsequently improving your notes and studying them effectively. Let's consider each step in a bit more detail.

Step 1: Record

First, make sure you record what is being taught—but that doesn't mean writing everything down verbatim. As we have discussed, regardless of whether you use a laptop or write longhand, you should train yourself to get the main ideas in a lecture or class into your notes. Sometimes an instructor will give you an outline or prompts to guide your note-taking. Even if they do not, document the content in order. If a slideshow is presented in class, use the slides to guide what you write down. Pay special attention for information, such as a definition, that is not in the book (this another good reason to read the material ahead of class).

Then, do not stop writing once you record what is on the screen or slide. Most often, good faculty make connections with the content verbally, through storytelling or other examples. They may provide an example or an application of a concept or a connection to a different part of the course. Write down these connections in your own words. In addition, sometimes a student will ask a question, and, while the instructor is responding, some students take this opportunity to check email or send a text. Do not make that mistake. If a student has a question, see if you can answer it yourself, in your head. If you can correctly recall it, then answering for yourself will actually help you remember the answer in the future (for more details, see Chapter 4). If you cannot answer it, you should jot down the question and answer; this may help you learn the material better.

The *Outline method*, the *Matrix method*, and the *Cornell method* are three common note-taking strategies. If you did not know there were various strategies, your default go-to method likely resembles the Outline method, with a few organizational innovations. With the Outline method, you list main headings near the top of the page and use subheadings to separate and organize your material. To make the information more visibly organized, some people use indentations. This method has been associated with better recall of information but is not as helpful as some other, more complex methods.

With the Matrix method, you create a table wherein the main topics are listed along the top of the page and a row of subtopics goes down the left side of the page. If you were taking notes on this chapter using the Matrix method your main topics would likely include "Functions of Notes," "Ways to Take Notes," and "Research Examples." "Types," "Advantages," and "Disadvantages" would be listed along the left side. Then, you would take notes in each box. One benefit of using this approach is that it is easy to read and helps you make connections across concepts. One downside is that predicting what categories you will need for a lecture may be difficult. Therefore, to reiterate, this type of note-taking is easier to do when taking notes from a text.

Perhaps the most common model suggested for student note-taking is the Cornell method. In the Cornell method, you set up your notebook as shown in Figure 3.4 (Pauk & Ross, 2013). You draw a vertical line down the left side about 25% to 33% of the way in. When you take notes in class, you write only to the right of the line. After class, you add headings and organizational elements. You can also jot down points on which you were unclear or that you think you missed. The bottom section is where you summarize the lecture.

All three note-taking methods allow you to record your notes well, and each one varies in the extent to which you can modify or

FIGURE 3.4. A Format for Using the Cornell Method for Note-Taking

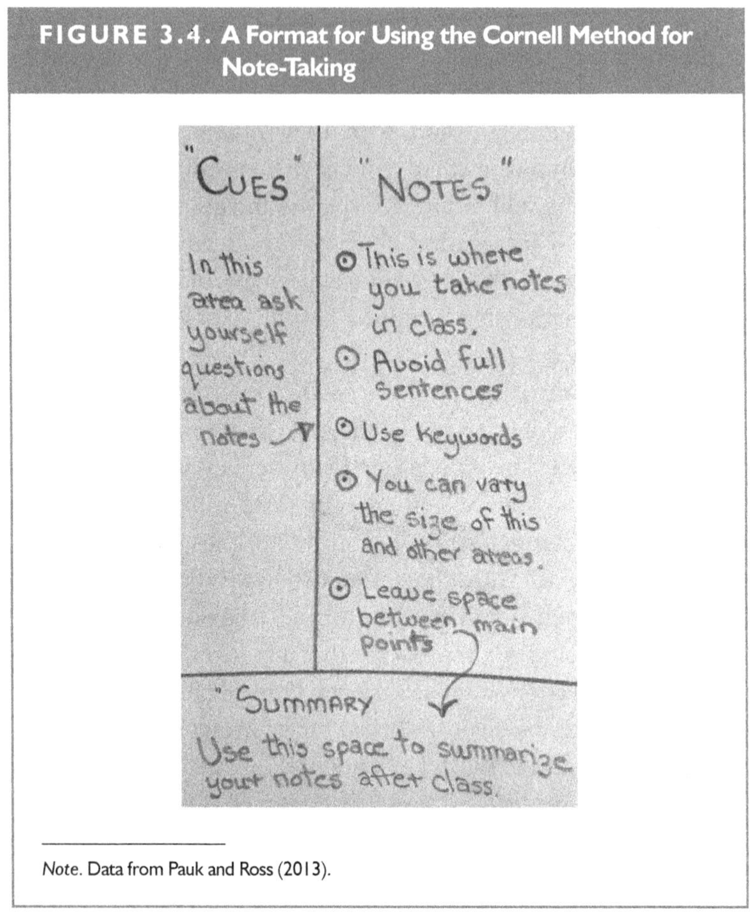

"Cues"
"Notes"
In this area ask yourself questions about the notes
This is where you take notes in class.
Avoid full sentences
Use keywords
You can vary the size of this and other areas.
Leave space between main points
"Summary
Use this space to summarize your notes after class.

Note. Data from Pauk and Ross (2013).

revise your notes after the lecture. This will become important in the second step of note-taking.

Thus far, we have urged you to take down "key points" or the "main points." That is all easy to say, but how exactly do you *know* what the main or key points are? If you are lucky, your instructor may clearly provide a list of key points on a slide to start or end class, on your Learning Management System (e.g., Canvas), or on a handout. That does not happen often because many faculty believe pulling main points from a lecture is a skill that students should develop. However, we realize that this skill has to be learned, and it takes practice. So, here are some guidelines. If you practice these, you will be able to better identify key points in a lecture:

- **Be prepared for class.** Check the syllabus so you know what the topic of the day is, read or skim your assigned readings so will recognize any new terms used, and look over your notes from the previous class so you can make connections.
- **Watch for clues.** Instructors often start with an overview or an agenda for the day and then recap material before moving on. They may also repeat a point. Any material in a recap or that is repeated is something to be written down.
- **Listen for clues.** Instructors often change their tone, their volume, or their rhythm when they cover important points. They may pause for effect, lower or raise their voice to highlight a point, or slow down to define a concept. You should listen for these clues; they signify important points.
- **Collect the flags.** All instructors use some verbal flag to identify key points. Sometimes it is the direct "This is important"; other times, it can be more subtle, such as "Remember this" or "This will return." Flags such as "however," "for example," and "in contrast" may signal important information as well.

Step 2: Revise

Although most note-taking research has focused on the first and last Rs in the R3 method, it is now clear that another R needed to be sandwiched in between. Empirically tested by Luo et al. (2016), the revision of notes is a critical element. Revision can take many forms. The key is to look at your notes shortly after you have taken them.

Optimally, you should revise them right after class, but if you have something else to do right after class, consider setting aside some time to look at your notes on the same day or at least during the first study session scheduled after class (which should be relatively soon after the class, anyway; see Chapter 5 for ideas on scheduling study sessions). Here is some motivation to revise your notes: Studies spanning almost 100 years have shown that, on average, students capture only 35% of lecture content in their notes (Peverly & Wolf, 2019), which is a little better than the 11% found in one study discussed before (i.e., Raver & Maydose, 2010). Revising may help you capture more content. When you revise your notes, you should try to identify any gaps. Does something seem missing or incomplete? Can you make sense of what you wrote down? These are great questions to ask yourself when you first review your notes; they are a form of self-explanation (which we discuss in further detail in Chapter 6).

> *Look at your notes shortly after you have taken them. Does something seem missing or incomplete? Can you make sense of what you wrote down? Organizing your notes and transforming your professor's words into your own help you recall the material later.*

If you feel that you have a hard time copying everything down, fear not. You are not alone. In fact, most adults do not have the sensory capabilities to record complete lecture notes. Adults write, on average, 22 words a minute and type 33 words a minute, but they can listen to about 210 words a minute (Karat et al., 1999). The average lecture contains 100 to 125 words a minute (Wong, 2014). Thus, giving yourself time to revise after class helps out your otherwise-challenged sensory system during class.

In addition, when you take time to revise your notes you can use the revision as an opportunity to retrieve the information from memory. This process of retrieval is one of the classic tricks to being a Study Champion, and we have a whole chapter (Chapter 5) devoted to retrieval. When you retrieve information, you can add your own words to help you make more sense of what you wrote down while also filling in missing pieces. By adding information, you make your notes more comprehensive and allow for a deeper processing of the material. When you organize your notes and transform your professor's words into your own, you are elaborating on the material in a way that can help you recall it later. This is also a good time to correct mistakes. If you find mistakes, missing parts, or sections you think are incorrect, go talk to your instructor.

Note that you do not have to wait until after class, or rely on your own memory, to revise notes. If there are pauses in the lecture (say, if the instructor is setting up a video or preparing a demonstration), you can use that time to revise the notes you just took. In addition, you can make a point to compare your notes with a classmate's, either during a pause or soon after class. It is good practice to check your notes against a classmate's to ensure you took accurate ones. A classmate can also come in handy when you review.

Step 3: Review

Note that the third R in the R3 model is not reREAD but reVIEW. When you review, you are not passively skimming the notes you took but actively looking at them with a critical eye. You are like the reviewer of a scholarship or job application: You are asking the question "How good is this?" In this part of the process you do not add more material (as in the Revise part) but instead work to solidify the information in memory. The chapters in Part II of this book address how to go about effectively studying your notes so as to better understand and remember them.

In Practice: Fine-Tune Your Note-Taking

Similar to the self-assessment above, the assessment presented next will help you gauge the extent to which you use evidence-based best practices to get the most out of your note-taking (Chen, 2021). Think again about a specific class you are taking right now. Think about the extent to which you do each of the following items in the following list. This time, we have left the section names in so you can see what you need to practice and get better at. You can consider this your checklist of how to become a better note-taker once you have mastered the items in the previous assessment (the Start Now questions).

Elaboration:

1. ______ I read the relevant chapters in the textbook and add supplementary information to my lecture notes using my own words.
2. ______ I mark/highlight the important points in my lecture notes by underlining or using annotations.
3. ______ To facilitate memory, I write down examples that I am familiar with next to the important points explained by the lecturer.
4. ______ I include additional explanations next to important points or concepts.
5. ______ I arrange the key words I have written down during the lecture into sentences or content that I understand.

Organization:

1. ______ I organize the contents of my notes into an outline or chart.
2. ______ I integrate the contents of the textbooks and my notes and then note the overall structure of the content.
3. ______ I use numbers to annotate the order or context of the contents of my notes.
4. ______ I read the relevant chapters in the textbooks and then note the relationship between the main topics in my notes.
5. ______ I refer to the outline in the textbooks or handouts and then reorganize the contents of my notes.

Help-Seeking:

1. _____ I consult my classmates or the lecturer to confirm the meaning of the contents of my notes.
2. _____ I compare my notes with those of my classmates and add any main points that I may have left out into my notes.
3. _____ I consult my classmates or the lecturer to supplement any areas that I did not completely write down during the lecture.
4. _____ I consult my classmates or the lecturer to clarify any areas in my notes that I am still unclear about and then make the necessary revisions.

Note. From "In-Class and After-Class Lecture Note-Taking Strategies," by P.-H. Chen, 2021, *Active Learning in Higher Education*, 22(3), pp. 245–260. (https://doi.org/10.1177/1469787419893490).

The key to taking good notes, whether on a computer or on paper, is to be focused. Even if you write longhand but are also texting or otherwise distracted, you may still miss key parts of the lecture. However, if your mind is free to focus on the lecture and make connections among it, the readings, and life, you will remember more.

Deciding how to take notes goes beyond just utility and speed. Given how much time we all spend with technology, you may want to take longhand notes and give yourself a technology break. As with the paper planning calendar we suggested in Chapter 2, this is a great opportunity to get a neat notebook. Pick something you will enjoy looking at, carrying about, and using. Picking a distinctly different notebook for each class can help keep things separate in your mind as well.

Do not be afraid to use paper and illustrate ideas visually. In some classes, the instructor will draw a diagram or show a flowchart on the screen. Although that would be difficult to capture on a computer unless you were able to take a photo of it, diagrams are easier to capture when you write on paper. The example in the end-of-chapter summary visual shows you how good-looking notes can be and gives an example of the work of one of our students, Paige Herrboldt, who drew all the images for our chapter summaries, showing how she first jots down the key points from a class and then illustrates her notes as a way to elaborate and organize them.

HUDDLE UP

Taking notes serves many different purposes and is an important skill to learn. Good note-taking skills can serve you well, even beyond higher education. Whether you are on a jury, such as in our chapter-opening vignette, or if you are attending a seminar or conference for work, your ability to take good notes ties directly to what you remember.

Different classes may call for different note-taking strategies. See which strategies work better for you. If you are wondering whether you are capturing the most important content, consider having your instructor look over your notes, or check out notes that your other classmates are taking. Taking good notes will typically just be the beginning of meeting your learning goals. But if you have great notes, you are on your way to studying like a champion, which involves using effective study strategies to understand and remember those notes. This is the focus of the next chapters.

Key Training Tips

- Study Champions take organized notes that help them capture what is discussed in class but also serve as an aid to elaboration on important points.

- Sticking Your Landing requires you to find the best note-taking method from the variety out there that can help you capture content and serve as a study aid.
- Go For the Gold by completing your reading assignments before class.

Go for the Gold With an Advanced Reading

Peverly, S. T., & Wolf, A. D. (2019). Note-taking. In J. Dunlosky & K. A. Rawson (Eds.), *The Cambridge handbook of cognition and education* (pp. 320–355). Cambridge University Press.

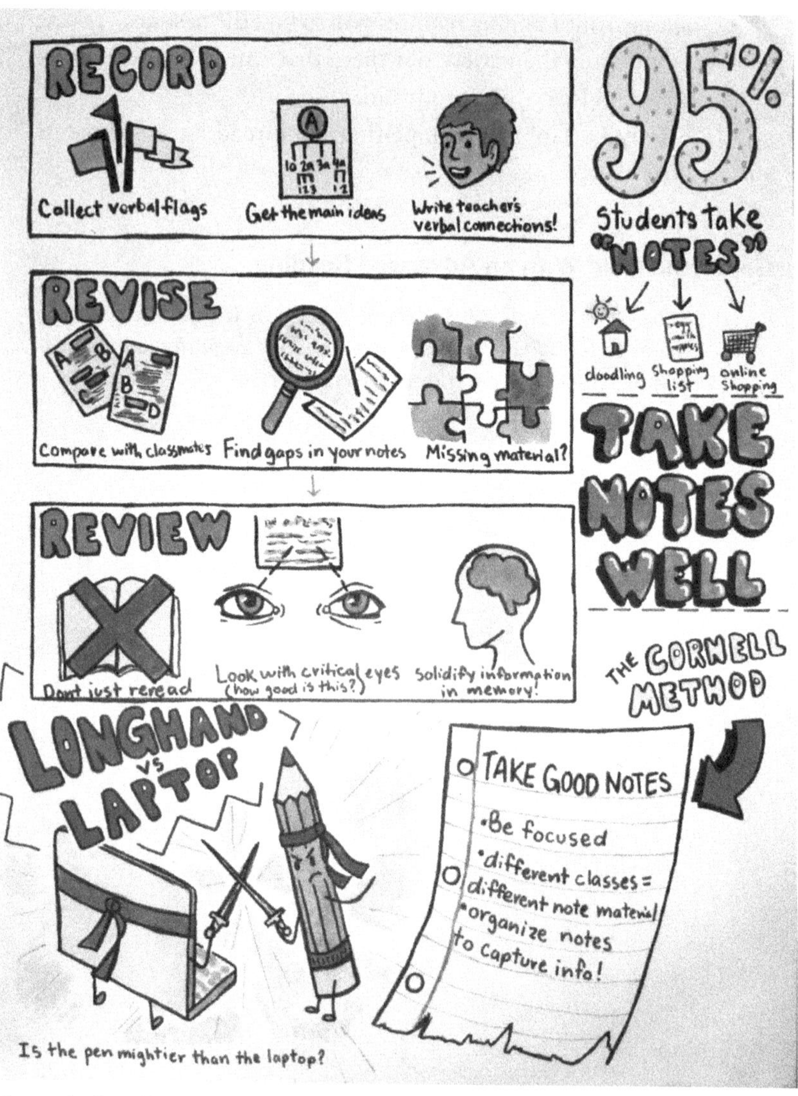

Drawing by Paige Herrboldt. Printed with permission.

II

STRATEGIES

CHAPTER 4

SPACING IT OUT

In this chapter, you will learn

- whether you are an Early Bird, a Crammer, or a Spacer;
- how other students approach studying for courses; and
- four key steps to schedule your study sessions like a champion.

Jeremiah and Sonia are conscientious students and want to do well in their Introductory Psychology class. So, they did what most faculty always tell students to do: Start studying early! They took great notes and followed the guidelines of good planning, they made sure to sleep well, and they practiced other healthy behaviors. They made sure that they studied their assigned chapters and notes multiple times a week, and when midterms rolled around both of them expected a strong grade. Unfortunately, Jeremiah and Sonia both earned low Cs on the midterm exam, and, perhaps not surprisingly, both of them were shocked when they found out. What went wrong?

To answer this question, please begin by taking a moment to think about and reflect on something you are really good at. Perhaps you are a skilled dancer or excellent at video games; maybe you were one of the better musicians at your school or a pretty good basketball player. Almost everyone is accomplished at something.

Now, here's the vital question: How did you develop your skills? No one was born being excellent at anything, and certainly no one achieves excellence when first beginning something new. So, how do people become accomplished? The answer to this question is universal because in every case of expertise, a common foundation is *spaced practice*.

WHAT IS SPACED PRACTICE?

With respect to studying like a champion, spaced practice involves studying some course material you need to learn and then coming back to restudy that same material at least one other day. When developing the fundamentals of playing a sport or an instrument, spaced practice seems natural. For instance, if you are trying to learn how to make free throws for a basketball game, then practicing free throws on one day and coming back a day later to practice dribbling would not constitute spaced practice. To become a sharpshooter, you have to practice free throws again the next day and likely on many (many) other days. Although this seems like common sense, most people do not realize that the same spaced practice that can help anyone learn a skill (e.g., playing a video game or the violin) is also essential for studying like a champion and excelling in college.

Now consider the case of three students who are preparing for their first exam in Introductory Psychology. The classes are held on Mondays, Wednesdays, and Fridays, and, as illustrated in Figure 4.1, the Spacer and the Early Bird both begin studying 3 weeks before the first exam, and they both spend about the same time studying during each study session (around 2 hours). The Spacer begins each session by studying the content presented in the class the day before; during Monday of Week 1, the instructor introduced the first half of the history lecture (History 1, in Figure 4.1), so the Spacer spends some time studying History 1 on Tuesday. However, after

FIGURE 4.1. Examples of Three Schedules

	The Spacer	The Early Bird	The Crammer
Week 1			
Tuesday	Study History 1	Study History 1	↓
Thursday	Study History 2 Review History 1	Study History 2	↓
Week 2			
Tuesday	Study Experimental Method 1 Review History 2	Study Experimental Method 1	↓
Thursday	Study Experimental Method 2 Review History 1 Review Experimental Method 1	Study Experimental Method 2	↓
Week 3			
Tuesday	Study Neuron 1 Review Experimental Method 2 Review History 2	Study Neuron 1	↓
Thursday	Review all content	Review all content	Study all content

Friday: Exam 1. Covering History 1 & 2, Experimental Methods 1 & 2, and Neuron 1 studying this newly introduced material, the Spacer then returns to review and restudy earlier material. For instance, on Thursday of the first week the Spacer begins by studying the second half of the history lecture that was presented on Wednesday (History 2) and then reviews History 1.

As new material is provided across a semester, the Spacer studies the new material and reviews as much of the older material as possible during each study session. In contrast, although the Early Bird also begins studying early, they focus only on material that had just been introduced in class. The Early Bird is spreading out study but is not spacing their practice, which involves coming back to restudy the previously studied material. Note also that both of these students review the material the evening before the exam, so in this way the Early Bird is also getting in some spaced practice (which is great), whereas the Spacer is getting yet another review of all the material. Both of these students markedly contrast the Crammer, who begins their first real study session an evening (or perhaps two) before the exam.

Here are a few questions to answer (honestly) to yourself before moving forward:

- Which of these students do you believe would do better on Exam 1?
- Who would remember more of the information if given a surprise cumulative exam over the material at the end of the semester?
- Perhaps most important, which one of these kinds of student best characterizes how you study? Are you a Spacer, an Early Bird, or a Crammer?

If you are a Spacer, congratulations! In other chapters, we discuss the most effective strategies you can use as you review previously studied materials. Jeremiah and Sonia were Early Birds, but they did not space their studying of the same material, so they would not benefit from the power of spaced practice. Even so, if you are an Early Bird as well, the great news is that all you need to do is organize your studying differently, so that you review previously studied material each study session in addition to studying any new material introduced in a course. If you are a Crammer, you can substantially improve your outlook by simply scheduling more spaced study sessions—you have a lot to gain from taking a different approach to studying!

> *The most effective way to study—spaced practice—involves studying some course material you need to learn and then coming back to restudy that same material at least one other day.*

Are most students Spacers, Early Birds, or Crammers? Well, in a large-scale survey, college students were asked about when they intended to study for upcoming exams; the results are shown in Figure 4.2. As illustrated by the solid line, many students *intended* to spread out their study—we do not know if they were going to review, like Early Birds or Spacers, but their intent was to begin studying long before the last evening available. Even here, however, most students intended to ramp up their study the night before the exam. After their exams, the same students were asked to report when they had actually studied and for how long. What is evident from the dashed line is that although many students intended to begin early, when the semester was in full swing, they had difficulties meeting their goals and ended up studying less than intended—they put off much of the studying until a day or two before the exam. Cramming the night before an exam is not necessarily bad, as long as you get enough sleep. However, the overall impact of your studying will be greatly improved if you not only get started early (like many students intend to do) but also use spaced practice.

FIGURE 4.2. Students' Reports of How Much Time They Intended to Study (and When They Planned on Studying) for Exams and Their Reports About How Much (and When) They Actually Studied

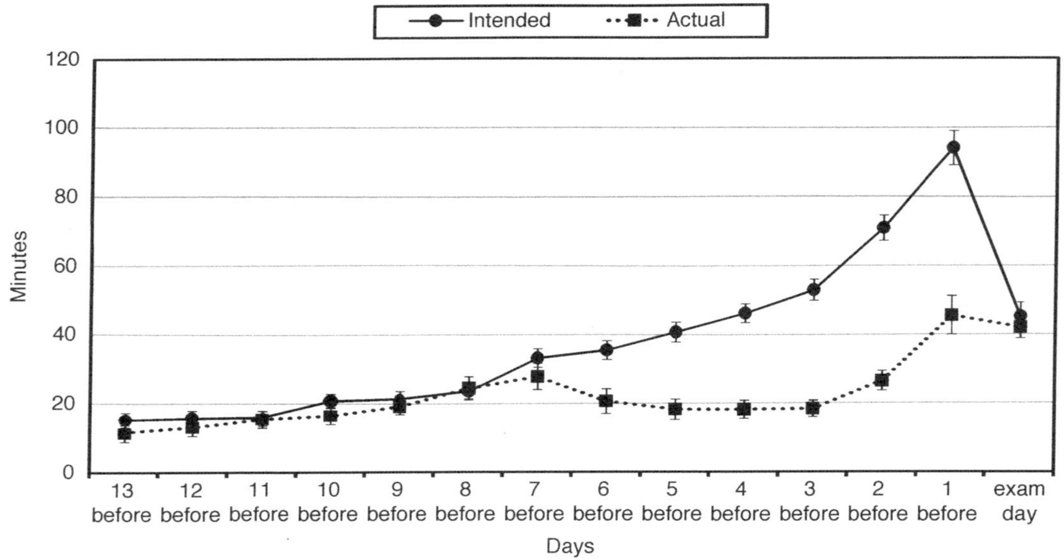

Note. From "The What, How Much, and When of Study Strategies: Comparing Intended Versus Actual Study Behavior," by R. Blasiman, J. Dunlosky, and K. Rawson, 2017, *Memory, 6*, p. 788. Copyright 2017 by Taylor & Francis. Reprinted with permission.

WHAT'S THE EVIDENCE? A LOOK INSIDE THE LABORATORY

Spaced practice is essential for studying like a champion, but how are we sure? Well, more than 100 years of research has demonstrated that long-term performance and retention increase dramatically after spaced practice as compared with massed—or crammed—practice. In 1885, Hermann Ebbinghaus conducted the first experimental studies on memory using himself as the only subject. With a series of clever experiments, he discovered that he learned simple verbal materials more quickly if he spaced his study of those materials across several days than if he massed (or crammed) his study during a single session. The results from hundreds of studies conducted since have established that performance will typically be better for students who are Spacers than for those who are Early Birds or Crammers, and, in many cases, the difference in performance is large (for historical and analytic reviews, see Cepeda et al., 2006, and Wiseheart et al., 2019). Spacing your study can really improve your learning and retention!

However, like some other students we have interviewed, you may argue, "Well, I would use spaced practice, but it doesn't work for me. I do much better if I just cram the night before an exam." If you hold this belief, however, know that it is incorrect—it is a common misconception that could arise from two sources. First, cramming the night before an exam may earn you a passing grade, which would naturally give you the false sense that cramming is a good study technique that would lead to durable learning. However, that's not true: If you only cram, then you will forget a lot of what you learned soon after you take the test, and you might even forget quite a bit beforehand, too. Second, the benefits of spaced practice are practically universal: It works for little white mice, for yellow buzzing bees, and for people with severe memory deficits, so it will definitely work for you. However, you need to use it correctly; we give advice about this later in this chapter. It is great to try out techniques to get a sense about how well they work for you, but, unfortunately, when you try out a technique or strategy but do not use it correctly, misconceptions about its effectiveness can arise. We sympathize, because sometimes it can be tricky to use a technique so that it will work like it should. However, as 100 years of research shows, spaced practice will work for you, and we will give you some concrete advice soon on how to harness its power.

Before we move on to consider a bit of evidence from research conducted in authentic classrooms—the research that is most relevant to you—we want to share a couple more thoughts about cramming. *Cramming* is essentially waiting to do most (or perhaps even all) of your studying the night before an exam, and we suspect in many cases this cramming session turns into an all-nighter, forcing those involved to forego a full night's rest. One study showed that most students—across multiple science disciplines—rely heavily on cramming for test preparation. The students in this investigation were enrolled in courses for which the learning materials were accessible online, so the researchers could observe when students were studying (Taraban et al., 1999). The majority of students waited until the evening before to do most of their studying—a classic case of cramming!

We highly recommend that you do not cram. It's fine to study the evening before an exam; it may calm your nerves, help you feel more comfortable with the material, and get you ready to go for the next day. However, if all you do is cram, and you do not use spaced practice to prepare, you run the risk of not performing to your potential. Cramming alone leads to quick forgetting, so if you have a cumulative exam at the end of the semester, you will retain little of what you have studied and may struggle to learn all the material presented in the course prior to that cumulative exam. Most important, if you do end up pulling an all-nighter (or even a partial one), your sleep may be disturbed. Getting a good night's sleep is essential for performing your best; this is a point that is so important that we return to it later in this book (Chapter 9).

WHAT'S THE EVIDENCE? A LOOK INSIDE THE CLASSROOM

We will describe in detail how to use the spaced practice technique (and many others) in the right way so that your studying will benefit. Before we do, however, consider one investigation, conducted in real classrooms, that demonstrates the benefits of spaced practice. Our aims for describing such investigations go beyond convincing you that spaced practice works—believe us, it does!—to also include illustrating a few ways that you could use spaced practice while learning your course materials. In this investigation, Gurung and Burns (2019) worked with more than 300 students (from nine different colleges and universities) to prepare for their exams in Introductory Psychology. Students were assigned to either study using spaced practice (Figure 4.3) or to practice in a more massed fashion; massed practice is typified by studying materials in a single session, but in this case students were simply not given any instructions on when to study and were expected to mass—or cram—most of their study soon before the exam. Also, students used either less or more retrieval practice when studying. Retrieval practice involves attempting to retrieve the sought-after materials from memory; in this study, students practiced retrieval by completing practice quizzes. We discuss retrieval practice in more detail in Chapter 5. For now, our take-home message pertains to the impact of spacing practice, and you can see the results for yourself in Figure 4.3: Exam performance was higher (by a letter grade) when practice was more spaced across time.

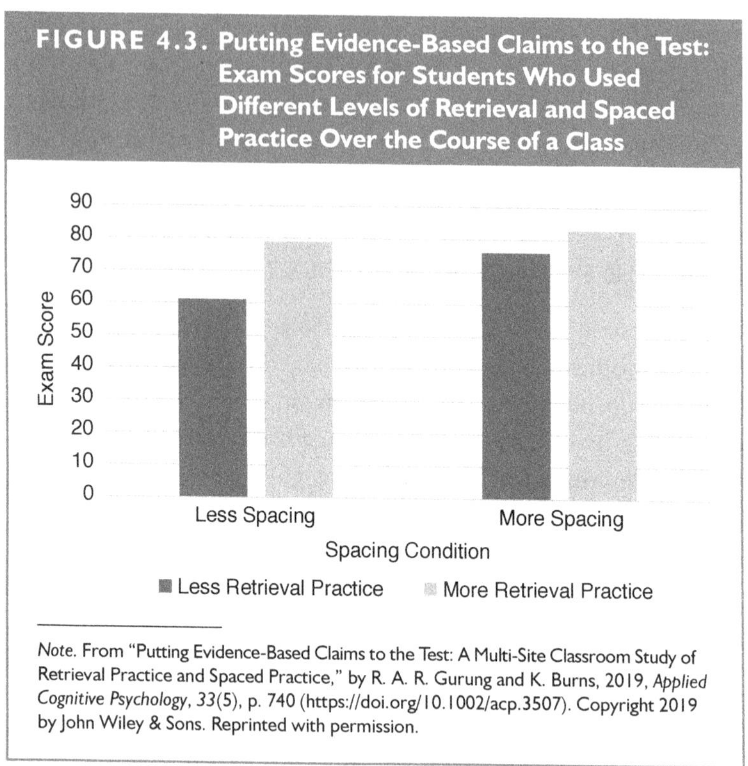

FIGURE 4.3. Putting Evidence-Based Claims to the Test: Exam Scores for Students Who Used Different Levels of Retrieval and Spaced Practice Over the Course of a Class

Note. From "Putting Evidence-Based Claims to the Test: A Multi-Site Classroom Study of Retrieval Practice and Spaced Practice," by R. A. R. Gurung and K. Burns, 2019, *Applied Cognitive Psychology, 33*(5), p. 740 (https://doi.org/10.1002/acp.3507). Copyright 2019 by John Wiley & Sons. Reprinted with permission.

TIPS FOR USING SPACED PRACTICE

Spacing your practice, although it is certainly helpful, is not enough. To take full advantage in meeting your learning objectives, you are going to have to do some planning and recordkeeping as you study (see Chapter 2). What follows is a detailed example showing how you could best use spaced practice to prepare for an exam over four chapters in an Introductory Biology course. Of course, spaced practice can be used in many ways, so we do not expect that you would follow all these details entirely; instead, we have attempted to provide enough details about how to use this technique so that you can effectively adapt it when you prepare for real exams.

In the sections that follow, you will learn

- how to use spaced practice during a study session and
- how to coordinate multiple spaced-practice study sessions.

First, we describe how you can use spaced practice during a single study session for new material, as if you were beginning to study your notes from a class lecture. We then discuss how you can coordinate multiple spaced-practice study sessions. The idea is to use shorter study sessions, around 1 to 2 hours long, multiple times per week, so that you can use spaced practice and other effective learning strategies that we introduce in later chapters to meet—and even exceed—your learning objectives. You will ultimately need to decide exactly how much time you can or want to put in for each course you take; the amount of time you will need to meet your goals may vary considerably depending on the difficulty level of a course. Nevertheless, our recommendations assume you are dedicated to studying like a champion by setting up a study schedule, managing your time, and rewarding yourself when you meet your studying goals.

An Example of Spaced Practice Within a Study Session

As an example, let's assume that you are taking an Introductory Biology course that meets twice per week, on Mondays and Wednesdays. You just had your first lecture, on the chemical basis of life. Your instructor lectured and presented some videos, and after the class you have about four pages of notes that include a great deal of information you will need to know for the first exam. The information may include the meaning of fundamental concepts, such as acids and bases, as well as the names of the most important structures, such as major molecules. You already have a lot of information to learn, and you have another lecture coming up in 2 days. Soon after the first lecture is a great time to begin using spaced practice, which will put you on the path to learning—and even mastering—this difficult material.

Step 1: Map Out a Study Schedule

What should you do first? To use spaced practice effectively, we highly recommend that you begin by mapping out a study schedule for the entire semester. To do this, figure out how many sessions you can spend studying biology per week, and then mark out a block of time in your calendar that will be dedicated to studying for this course. Perhaps you decide to schedule two 2-hour study sessions per week, one session on the day after each lecture. Of course, this may not be enough time for more difficult content (and may even be more than is necessary for easier content), so the idea is to begin with a reasonable schedule and then adjust it as needed. This two-session-a-week schedule reflects the example in Figure 4.1 that was used by both the Early Bird and the Spacer. But you want to be a Spacer and not just an Early Bird, so how should you proceed?

Step 2: Spacing Study Within the Study Session

Imagine now that you are sitting down for your first study session. We recommend reviewing your notes to make sure you understand them all. For any notes that you do not understand, mark them so that you remember to obtain further help. This is a great time to take out your highlighter—perhaps a color that signifies "I don't quite understand"—so that you remember to get clarification, either by reading the relevant portions of your textbook or asking your instructor to explain the confusing material again. When reviewing your notes, also be sure to highlight the most important content that you think you will need to learn—perhaps using a different color that signifies "I better know this for the exam." It turns out that initially reviewing your notes may take only about 30 minutes, so you finish well before your allotted time is over. What next?

During a 2-hour study session, this may be a great time to take a quick break. Stand up and walk around, and maybe do some jumping jacks and stretch. Taking just a few minutes for a quick break to do a physical activity appears to reinvigorate people so they get more out of the remainder of their study sessions. You also may decide to stop studying and go on to something else, perhaps because you feel that you have a good grasp of the material presented on the first day. Doing so, however, may not be the best idea. Because you were just presented that information in class, you may suffer from an illusion of knowing (the FoK in Chapter 1) when you go back to restudy it—most of the material will feel familiar, and such familiarity can lead anyone to believe they have a good understanding of it when in fact they actually have not yet learned the material well enough to retain it for an upcoming exam. Such familiarity can be short-lived and often does not mean that you actually understood and will retain the material.

To begin dealing with this problem, consider taking advantage of spacing your practice within a session. Instead of closing your notes, go back one more time to restudy what you just reviewed. This is meant to boost your learning of the material a bit more, and you will likely have the best results if your restudying involves using an effective learning strategy, such as self-explanation or retrieval practice (see Chapters 5 and 6 for details on these strategies). In other words, spaced practice is merely a schedule for how to practice—in this case, you schedule your time to practice the material across time both within and between study sessions. But how much should you restudy the material in a single study session?

It turns out that the research on spaced practice does not firmly answer this question, and we suspect that no golden rule exists for how many spaced-study attempts are best within a given study session. Do not worry, though, because if you use spaced practice effectively you will be returning to this same material a few more times during subsequent study sessions, in part because mastering the material in a single session would be difficult, just like it would be difficult to excel at a new video game during a single evening.

Step 3: Spacing Your Study Across Sessions

After your next lecture, on Wednesday, which went a bit deeper into molecular structure and covalent bonds, you sit down on Thursday for your next study session. You have about three pages of new notes to add to the notes you took during the previous lecture. Begin by reviewing your new notes, as discussed above; that is, mark what you do not understand as well as material you are pretty sure is most important to learn for your upcoming exam. Now that you have reviewed your most recent notes, you should go back to the beginning of your notes and restudy them all. By doing so, you will be spacing your study of the first day of notes across two sessions, and you will be spacing your study of the new notes within that study session. Even for the content that you studied across two sessions, you will still likely forget some of what you learned, so before your exam you should try to restudy it in at least one more spaced session.

How much spaced practice is enough? Again, it turns out that there is no definitive answer to this question. For content that is very difficult for you to learn, you may have to continue restudying it during every study session until you are sure you will not forget it. Other content may take only an extra session or two to master. The good news is that if you combine spaced practice (which is merely an approach about how to schedule your study sessions) with retrieval practice (which is an engaging and effective study technique that allows you to monitor your progress), then you will have a pretty good idea about how well you know the class materials and whether you need to restudy them in a subsequent session. This combination of strategies—that is, practice retrieving the same content until you correctly retrieve it, and doing so repeatedly across multiple study sessions—is called *successive relearning*.

Successive relearning is a powerful study technique, and we discuss it in more detail in Chapter 5; specifically, we tell you how to use successive relearning to accurately evaluate your progress and provide some advice on how to decide when you have studied enough.

Step 4: Practice Makes Perfect

After your next lecture, you simply repeat the preceding steps: Begin by reviewing your newest notes, and then return to the beginning of your notes and study everything again. By now, you may be thinking, "But after about the fifth or sixth lecture, I will have so many notes that I will not have the time to review them all during each study session." Don't worry: This concern will vanish as you properly manage your time and get comfortable using spaced practice. Moreover, after about the third or fourth study session you will have a good comprehension of the material from the first lecture (assuming you used an effective study technique, e.g., retrieval practice). Thus, you will need to spend less and less time reviewing the materials you have already studied across multiple sessions, which will leave you more time to review and study the new material. In fact, we suspect that you will be shocked at how well you can learn large amounts of course content using spaced practice.

To achieve such learning bliss, discipline will be required. You need to set up a schedule for all your study sessions and spend the time reviewing new material and restudying all the older material during each session. In Chapter 2, we provided you with many examples of how to best use a calendar to effectively plan. Without a calendar, it may be difficult to keep track of what you have already studied and when you need to restudy it. To help you make sure you stay motivated and earn your learning rewards, we have a bit more advice to offer: Consider setting weekly goals. Sit down at the beginning of each week to think about how successful you want to be for that week and what you can realistically achieve. Perhaps you realize that the coming week will be extra busy, so you decide that you would be happy if you completed only half of your study sessions. Or you may have a relatively light week, with little other work or outside activities to deal with. If so, maybe you can try to schedule a few more study sessions; that is, you may want to set even higher goals for a particular week. The idea is to develop weekly goals that are flexible, allowing you to juggle all your activities and meet all your learning objectives.

> *We highly recommend that you begin by mapping out a weekly study schedule for the entire semester. Then modify the schedule each week as needed on the basis of your other workload and activities.*

After you set up your weekly goals, we recommend you make specific plans on how to accomplish them. If you have several study sessions planned for a particular day, you should also consider planning when you will take breaks, where you will study, and what you will do if you are distracted by friends. If your friends do not have the same goals, plans, and discipline, they can undermine your best efforts with a simple question: "Do you want to go and hang out for a while?" Hanging out with friends is great but not if doing so gets in your way of studying like a champion and obtaining your own learning goals. So, have a plan for how you're going to answer them. In this case, a simple "I have a few things I need to do first, but let me know where to catch up with you" is a great way to stick to your study plans and still find time to keep your relationships strong.

Remember to Reward Yourself!

When you meet your goals (or come close enough), remember to reward yourself. In fact, going out with friends may be a great reward, so why not treat yourself after you have accomplished your daily or weekly study sessions? Everyone has something they find rewarding, be it hanging out with friends, taking a break to work out, watching a favorite show, or even reading the latest crime novel. Whatever motivates you, consider putting it on your calendar when you set your goals at the beginning of the week. Don't fret: As you use spaced practice (along with a few other study techniques we describe in Chapters 5 to 7), your added success will be motivating in its own right. You will simply want to use these techniques more (and with greater fidelity) as you begin to discover how well they can work. But why not also pat yourself on the back for a job well done? A great way to do that is to figure out how you will reward yourself at the end of a long day or week of studying.

HUDDLE UP

If you are like most people, you probably have relied little on spaced practice to study for your classes and instead relied heavily on cramming, waiting until the last couple days before an exam to begin studying. Even if you have done okay, we suspect that you are reading this book because you know that you can improve your studying skills and academic achievements. If so, you are right, and by relying more and more on spaced practice you will quickly see your efforts pay off with higher class grades and longer term retention of what you have studied. In other words, after you try out spaced practice and do so with fidelity, perhaps combining it with other study strategies, your effectiveness and efficiency as a student will improve.

With such optimism in mind, we consider one final question to close this chapter: Should you give up cramming—the virtual security blanket of students around the globe—altogether? We have two different answers to this question. If you view cramming as an extended session that goes late into the evening the night before the exam, then we do not recommend it. Get a good night's sleep, so you can be at your best when you take your exam the next day. However, if you view cramming as doing some last-minute studying the night before (or day of) an exam, then by all means, go for it! If you have already used spaced practice to prepare, then your final cramming session should be a relatively carefree review of what you already know, so it can give you further confidence (and perhaps reduce some anxiety) when you sit down to take that exam.

Key Training Tips

- Space out studying the same content over several days.
- Set weekly goals, scheduling two or more weekly study sessions for each class and restudying the same content multiple times across the spaced study sessions.

Go for the Gold With an Advanced Reading

Wiseheart, M., Küpper-Tetzel, C. E., Weston, T., Kim, A. S. N., Kapler, I. V., & Foot-Seymour, V. (2019). Enhancing the quality of student learning using distributed practice. In J. Dunlosky & K. A. Rawson (Eds.), *The Cambridge handbook of cognition and education* (pp. 550–584). Cambridge University Press.

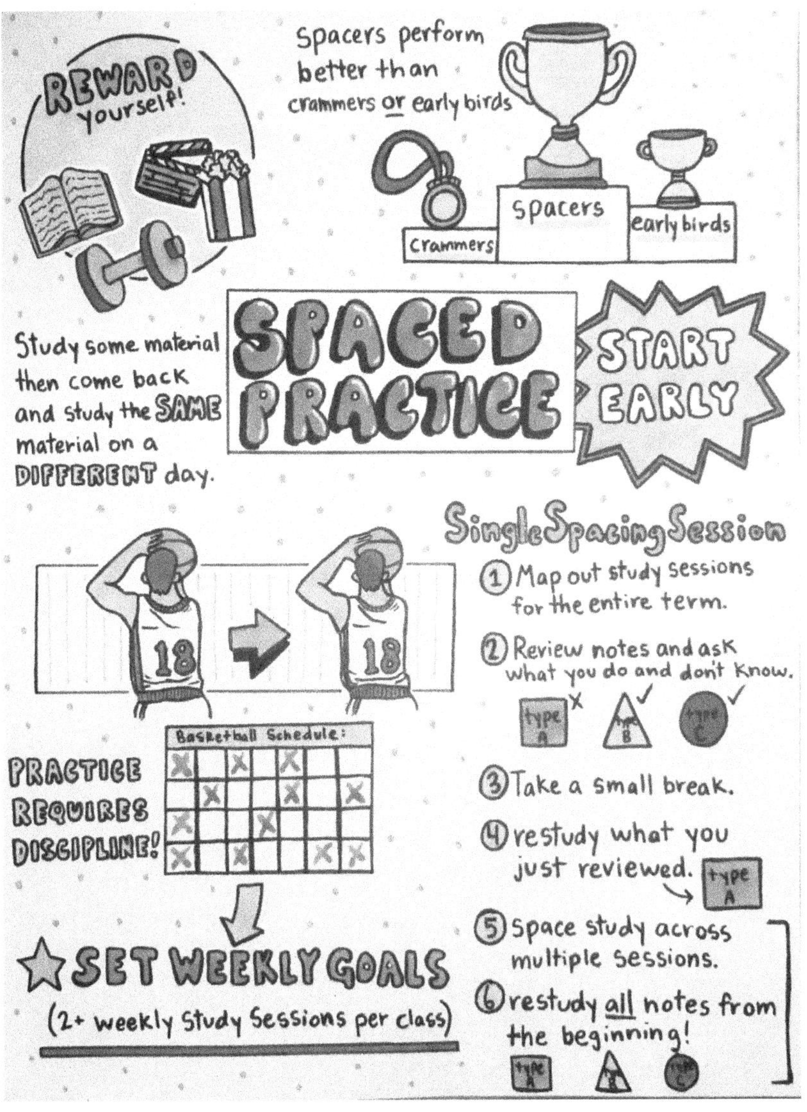

Drawing by Paige Herrboldt. Printed with permission.

CHAPTER 5

RETRIEVAL PRACTICE FOR MONITORING AND MASTERY

In this chapter, you will learn

- the power of trying to retrieve information from memory,
- why practicing until you succeed is essential for obtaining mastery, and
- how to get the most out of your notes and textbook by converting them into virtual flash cards.

Jenny, like many students, uses flash cards to help prepare for exams. She typically uses them to memorize foreign-language translation equivalents for her vocabulary tests. However, she also realizes that, although using flash cards helps her sometimes, it is not always so helpful. A difficulty Jenny is having is that she does not understand that flash cards are just tools that can be used in many different ways, and some of these ways promote success and others do not. Moreover, aside from using flash cards to learn foreign-language equivalents, when used appropriately they can be a much more valuable tool to master almost any course materials. Most important, when using flash cards does work, an active ingredient is the incorporation of retrieval practice into your study routine. In fact, using retrieval practice to help you monitor and improve your learning is one of the most powerful ways to study like a champion.

WHAT IS RETRIEVAL PRACTICE?

Retrieval practice simply means attempting to retrieve information from your memory that you would like to learn. The appropriate use of flash cards provides one example of retrieval practice because you are using retrieval practice whenever you test yourself by trying to recall a target from memory. This particular kind of test is called *cued recall* because a cue (e.g., "What does *chateau* mean?") prompts you to recall the correct target (in this case, the meaning of *chateau*: castle). As we explain shortly, you can also use other kinds of tests—such as multiple choice or free recall—to reap the benefits of retrieval practice.

Retrieval practice can help you learn a lot more than just word associations. For instance, trying to answer a question such as "What is operant conditioning?" or "How do you calculate acceleration?" without looking up the definition requires you to retrieve the answer from memory. This is also considered a cued recall test because the cue is the question itself. Although trying to retrieve longer definitions from memory can be frustrating, struggling to retrieve an answer, restudying the correct answer when you are wrong, and then struggling to retrieve it again later on until you finally retrieve it correctly is a powerful way to gain long-term retention of what you need to remember. However, to use retrieval practice like a Study Champion, you will need to know some specifics about why it works, when it works, and how best to make it work.

WHY IS RETRIEVAL PRACTICE AN EFFECTIVE STUDY TOOL?

As captured in the title of this chapter, retrieval practice can enhance your long-term retention in two ways (Roediger et al., 2011). First, practicing retrieval will help you *monitor* how well you are learning and make good decisions about what to restudy. Second, retrieval practice can also directly improve your retention of that information. *Monitoring* your learning involves assessing how well you are learning, and a great way to figure out whether you have learned something is to retrieve what you're trying to learn from memory. If you can't recall the information you are trying to learn, then there's a pretty good chance you won't be able to remember it later, when you need that information to answer test questions. Therefore, one reason flash cards can work so well is that they alert you to what you have not learned well enough to retrieve from memory, so you know to study that information again. With respect to the second benefit of retrieval practice, when you do correctly retrieve the sought-after information from memory, doing so directly enhances your retention of that information.

Retrieval practice is just another term for "practice test." And, well, who wants to take an anxiety-provoking test? The good news is that when you practice retrieving on your own, you may experience less anxiety because no stakes are involved. Also, if you take enough practice tests and use retrieval practice to monitor your progress toward mastery, you may even become less anxious when you take high-stakes exams. You may have noticed yourself that the forms of retrieval practice we have mentioned are essentially practice tests. Therefore, it should be no surprise that you can take different kinds of tests and still benefit from doing so.

When we teach, we use retrieval practice in class. Both of us often start class by asking our students a question relating to material covered in the week before. Sometimes we ask a question from the reading due for the day. We give our students some time to monitor whether they can remember the answer and make sure everyone gives it a try before we share the answer. Our students love it, and in fact most of them want us to do more of it in class. The great news is that you can do this yourself even without your instructor's help.

As we noted earlier, cued recall is a common type of test that you can easily use—just ask yourself a question and try to generate the answer from memory. Multiple-choice tests, which are commonly used by teachers to evaluate their students' knowledge, can also be used. Of course, developing your own multiple-choice tests can take a great deal of time and may be rather difficult to do, but many textbooks include practice quizzes that you can use. In some of our classes, students get together and create quizzes using free programs such as Quizlet (https://quizlet.com). Have a retrieval practice party (or study session)!

HOW MUCH DO YOU USE RETRIEVAL PRACTICE?

Before we discuss some evidence that showcases the power of retrieval practice, take a moment to answer this question: How often do you use retrieval practice in a typical day?

Many people do not realize just how much they rely on retrieval practice. Let's consider two examples. First, did you drive to school today? Taking the correct route is a form of retrieval practice, and the reason you can drive to school or work without thinking about it is that you've retrieved the route so often that you can practically do it in your sleep. Turning down the wrong street and getting lost indicates that you need to pay closer attention to that part of the route next time. Second, when you relax in the evening, do you play any video games or perhaps practice your favorite instrument? If you do either, then you are involved in a great deal of retrieval practice.

We talk to a lot of students who are really (really) good at video games, and why they are so good has to do with the magic of (spaced) retrieval practice. In particular, they need to retrieve the correct information about how to win a particular level of a game and practice retrieving the correct series of hand movements to achieve their goals within the gaming environment. When people engage in such retrieval practice—even if it's as low stakes as driving to the store—day after day, it is no surprise that they become much better. The bottom line is that you probably take advantage of retrieval practice a great deal every day, but you just don't realize it. This insight is critical because what you are naturally taking advantage of to excel in many everyday and past-time activities can be used equally well to prepare for exams in your classes. In fact, to study like a champion, you will need to rely heavily on retrieval practice as you work toward any of your learning objectives.

WHAT'S THE EVIDENCE? A LOOK INSIDE THE LABORATORY

Aside from research on the spacing effect, retrieval practice is one of the most frequently investigated techniques for improving students' memory, learning, and comprehension. But how, exactly, do researchers test whether retrieval practice works? Of course, almost any research that focuses on understanding people's memory and learning will involve some form of test, but for most memory research the test is used to measure people's memory *after* they have studied. For studying like a champion, however, the important insight is that when people take a test, the test itself not only measures their memory but also actually *enhances* their memory for it. This claim is supported by more than 100 years of research. Taking a test—or using retrieval practice—works, and it can work really well, too. But what exactly does it mean for retrieval practice "to work"?

To help you understand the answer to this question, consider an exemplary investigation conducted by Butler (2010), who had college students study a text passage—approximately 1,000 words long—about a complicated scientific process, such as how bats use echolocation. After studying the passage, the students then had a chance to learn the facts and concepts from some parts of the passage better, using retrieval practice. For such practice retrieval, cued recall tests were administered in which the students would be asked questions such as "How many bat species are there in the world?" (fact) and "How does echolocation help bats determine the size and location of prey?" (concept). After they attempted to answer a question, the students were presented with the portions of the passage that included the correct answers.

For other portions of the passage, the students reread the same excerpts without practicing retrieval. A critical part of this procedure is that the time spent on each method of studying was the same for all students. The final test comprised a new set of questions that required the students to apply what they learned from the passage. For instance, they may have been asked how a bat can determine whether an insect is moving toward or away from them, which was not explicitly covered in the passage but can be answered if the students understood how bat echolocation works. What did Butler (2010) find?

As shown in Figure 5.1, final test performance (across three different experiments) was about 20% higher when students were tested on the passages than when they just restudied them, regardless of whether the questions were about the facts or the concepts. Remember, students used the same amount of time whether they tested themselves or merely restudied, so although testing feels more difficult than just rereading the information you need to learn, it is a more effective study strategy and a better use of your time. The idea is to first test yourself; when you answer correctly, you'll be improving your retention of the material, and not answering correctly indicates that you do need to go back to restudy what you couldn't retrieve.

> *Although testing feels more difficult than just rereading the information you need to learn, it is a more effective study strategy and a better use of your time.*

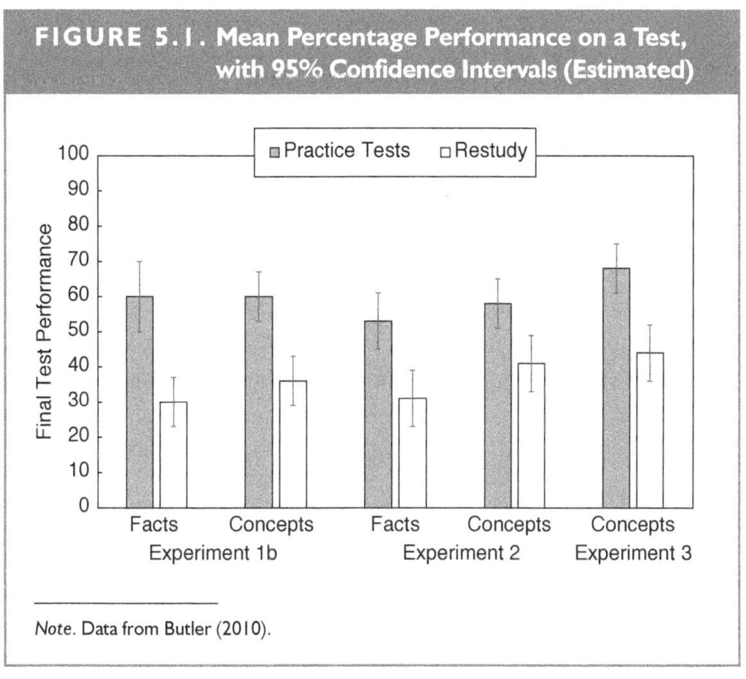

FIGURE 5.1. Mean Percentage Performance on a Test, with 95% Confidence Intervals (Estimated)

Note. Data from Butler (2010).

Research on what is called *test-enhanced learning*—because taking tests can enhance your learning—has been increasing, in part because education researchers have realized the great potential of harnessing retrieval practice to improve student achievement. In fact, in the past several decades retrieval practice has been shown to enhance learning across a broad range of people, materials, and exams. The following list is not exhaustive but is meant to give you a sense of the broad benefits of using retrieval practice:

- It has worked for children, college students, older adults, adults with aphasia, and adults with attention-deficit/hyperactivity disorder.

- It has helped people learn simple associations (e.g., foreign-language vocabulary), the content of text passages, definitions that are foundational to introductory courses, and the steps involved in scientific processes and mathematics.
- It has been shown to not only improve people's memory for the tested content but also enhance their understanding of it and their ability to apply what they have learned in new contexts.

The point of this list is straightforward: Including retrieval practice in your studying toolkit is essential because it holds much promise in improving your memory, learning, and comprehension of whatever you are studying. This is the case regardless of who you are, what you are studying, or how you ultimately will want to use what you have learned.

WHAT'S THE EVIDENCE? A LOOK INSIDE THE CLASSROOM

Classroom research on retrieval practice typically falls into one of two categories: Either an instructor administers some kind of practice test during each class to evaluate the degree to which in-class testing can enhance learning, or students test themselves outside of class, and then the impact of those practice tests is examined. In this section, we look at the first kind of classroom research, and then we touch on research relevant to taking the best advantage of practice retrieval when studying on your own.

In a course on Brain and Behavior, students took review quizzes that were meant to help them prepare for a high-stakes exam (Thomas et al., 2018). All of the review quizzes consisted of short-answer questions that were about facts or involved the application of concepts. For instance, on a review quiz about the cerebral cortex, an example of a fact-based question would be "The neocortex has a cytoarchitecture made up of what?" Meanwhile, an example of an applied question would be "You're looking at a small piece of brain tissue under a microscope. What distinctive organization would tell you this is neocortex?" (from Appendix A in Thomas et al., 2018). All students received both kinds of quiz questions on various topics. On the class exam all the questions were multiple choice, and whereas some of the questions were about the material covered on the review quizzes (e.g., the neocortex), other material was included that was not covered during review. The class exam included both fact-based questions and applied questions, so a student who answered a fact-based question about the neocortex during review would have to answer a conceptual question about it on the exam. Exam performance is presented in Figure 5.2, and a few outcomes are notable.

First, exam performance was better when students took a quiz on the content, whether the quiz was on facts or application (the two shaded bars in Figure 5.2), than when the content was not reviewed during a quiz (unshaded bars). Second, and unsurprisingly, students did the best when the kind of review quiz matched the kind of exam question; that is, reviews involving fact-based questions led to better performance on exam questions that asked for facts rather than applications, and vice versa. Finally, even for mismatches, review quizzes benefited students' exam performance; that is, even when they had review questions that covered facts, attempting to answer those review questions boosted later performance on application questions (as compared with not being quizzed over the material). This represents just one of many classroom demonstrations that have shown the power of retrieval practice for boosting performance for different kinds of students, classes, and exams (for a review, see Agarwal et al., 2021).

HOW TO USE SUCCESSIVE RELEARNING

Successive relearning is an incredibly powerful learning technique in large part because it combines the powers of two other effective approaches to learning: retrieval practice and spaced practice,

FIGURE 5.2. Exam Performance as a Function of the Kind of Essay Question Students Took During the Review Quiz (Either Not Quizzed, Factual Quiz, or Application Quiz) and the Type of Question on the Exam (Either Factual or Application)

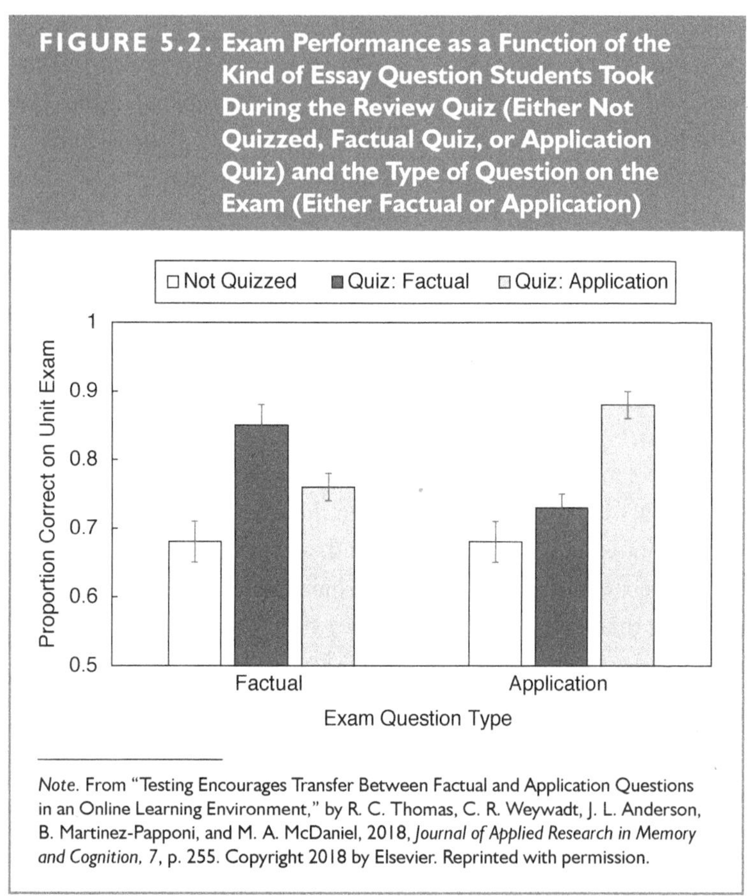

Note. From "Testing Encourages Transfer Between Factual and Application Questions in an Online Learning Environment," by R. C. Thomas, C. R. Weywadt, J. L. Anderson, B. Martinez-Papponi, and M. A. McDaniel, 2018, *Journal of Applied Research in Memory and Cognition, 7*, p. 255. Copyright 2018 by Elsevier. Reprinted with permission.

which were discussed in Chapter 4. Put more specifically, successive relearning first entails trying to retrieve the correct answer or response to a test prompt, examining feedback to evaluate whether your response is correct, and if it is not, then studying it again and repeating all the steps described earlier until you retrieve all the correct responses for a given set of materials. In this case, you would be *learning to a criterion* of one correct response, and the goal is to continue practice in a given study session until you meet that criterion.

You may be familiar with this procedure if you have ever used flash cards: You begin with a deck of cards that have a cue (or question prompt) on one side and the correct answer on the other. You then test yourself and study the answer for each card in turn. If you correctly recall an answer, you place that card aside, but if you don't correctly recall it you put the card at the back of the stack. That is the retrieval practice aspect of successive relearning. Then, you keep going through your stack of cards until you have retrieved each answer correctly once (i.e., you have met a criterion of one correct retrieval). You need to use multiple cards per stack so that if you miss a question and restudy its answer, a few minutes elapse before you test yourself again on that content. This practice allows for spaced practice of the material within a study session.

This procedure—which involves continuing to practice retrieving responses until you correctly recall them—is just the first step in successive relearning. The next step is to go through the procedure again—with the same material—on one or more other study sessions. Put differently, after you finish a particular stack of cards, you need to pick that same stack up a couple more times, and it is best if you can space those sessions across several days. The reason for going back to *relearn* the stack is because even after you can correctly recall answers to questions, you will forget some—perhaps many—of those answers. In other words, a single successful retrieval attempt does not mean that you have mastered that content, so you need to go back.

Using successive relearning to learn simple associations is rather straightforward, and it turns out that many students report using flash cards extensively in their second-language courses. What many students do not realize is that flash cards (or an equivalent) can be successfully used to learn other material, including complicated definitions and concepts, sequences of steps involved in a process, longer texts and descriptions about science and history, and much more. Unfortunately, using successive relearning to effectively study these more complex materials does pose some challenges. To help you understand these challenges, in Figure 5.3 we have included a flow chart of the steps involved in successive relearning. This figure simply puts the steps described above in a pictorial format, and in the paragraphs that follow we briefly touch on each step to highlight the challenges that may arise when you are using this technique for anything beyond simple associations.

Setting Up Practice Tests

Although the first step listed for successive relearning is simply testing yourself, you may need to set up the tests first. As we have mentioned, flash cards should have a cue on one side and the answer on the other. This will work for anything from simple word pairs to complex information such as lists. You likely already know how to build and use flash cards for simple associations, and the same approach works for more complex materials. Let's consider a few examples. For complex definitions (e.g., the definition of *bystander effect* or the definition of *individualism*), you write the term ("Bystander Effect") on one side of the flash card and the complete definition on the other side. If you are trying to learn lists (e.g., "What are all the facial nerves?"), then "Facial Nerves" would go on one side and the names of the nerves on the other. You can even use flash cards for lengthier materials, such as learning all the steps and processes involved in photosynthesis or the steps in an action potential. The key is to figure out what word, phrase, or question you want to use as the prompt for your retrieval attempt and then use that prompt to try to retrieve the answer from memory.

FIGURE 5.3. Flowchart Illustrating the Sequence of Steps for Successive Relearning

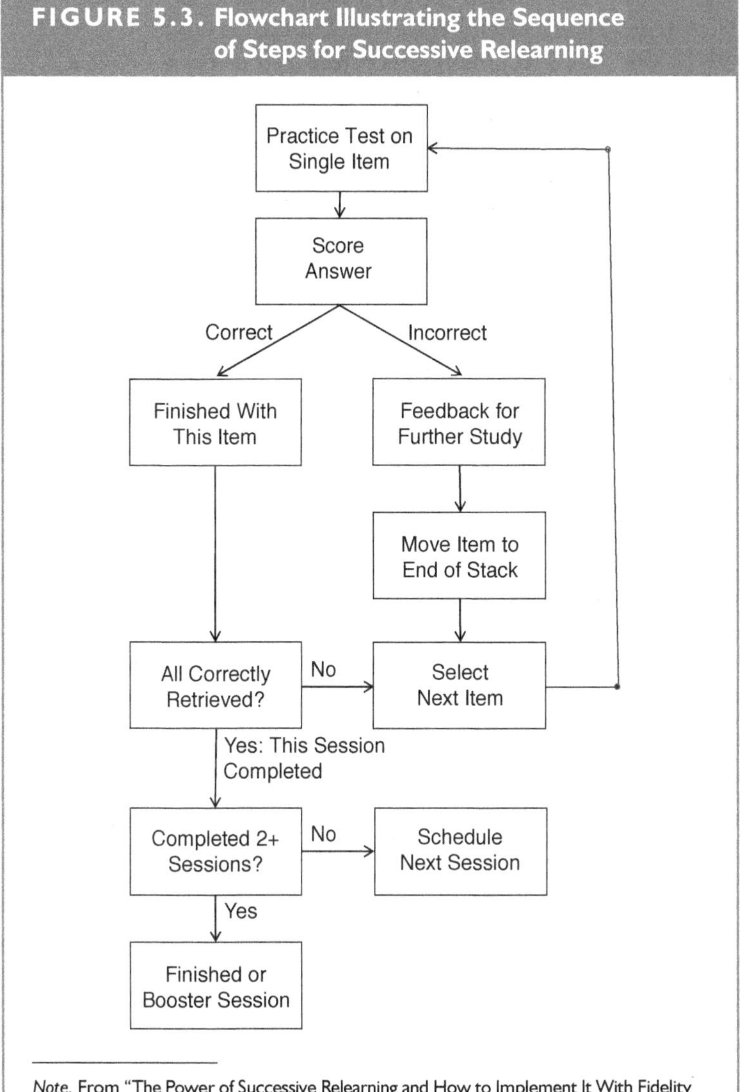

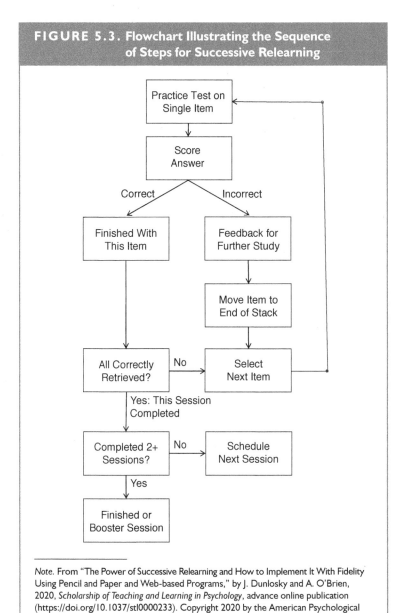

Note. From "The Power of Successive Relearning and How to Implement It With Fidelity Using Pencil and Paper and Web-based Programs," by J. Dunlosky and A. O'Brien, 2020, *Scholarship of Teaching and Learning in Psychology*, advance online publication (https://doi.org/10.1037/stl0000233). Copyright 2020 by the American Psychological Association.

> *Flash cards can be used to learn a lot of material, including complicated definitions and concepts, sequences of steps involved in a process, longer texts and descriptions about science and history, and much more.*

If you don't want to spend the extra time making flash cards, no problem. Many flash card programs are available online (many of them free), which can make this process easier (for a review of these programs with respect to how well they support successive relearning, see Dunlosky & O'Brien, 2020). Some programs will even let you share your cards with others, so why not pool your efforts with your friends and divide the work? Moreover, when studying in college, John never used flash cards but used successive relearning to master definitions, lists, and lengthy processes. Instead of taking the time to make all those cards, he simply put his hand over the definitions that appeared at the end of a textbook chapter and tested himself by trying to write down the correct definition on scrap paper.

With a pack of sticky notes, you can place one over each answer you want to retrieve and leave the word or phrase that you want to use as your retrieval prompt uncovered. As shown in Figure 5.4, using sticky notes may be particularly useful if you're trying to memorize the names of objects on a figure—in this illustration, the sticky notes are placed over the labels for the structures of the forebrain, and the student attempted to recall each structure name and then peeked behind the sticky note to grade their answers. The dates on the right side of the figure indicate each session in which the student used successive relearning, and the slash marks by each date reflect how many times the student needed to restudy until each answer was correctly recalled (note how the number of attempts dropped dramatically over just a few sessions). The sticky note approach works well because you can't accidentally peek at the correct answer, and you can write down how well you did (e.g., whether you recalled

FIGURE 5.4. Using Sticky Notes to Turn Your Textbook Into Functional Flash Cards

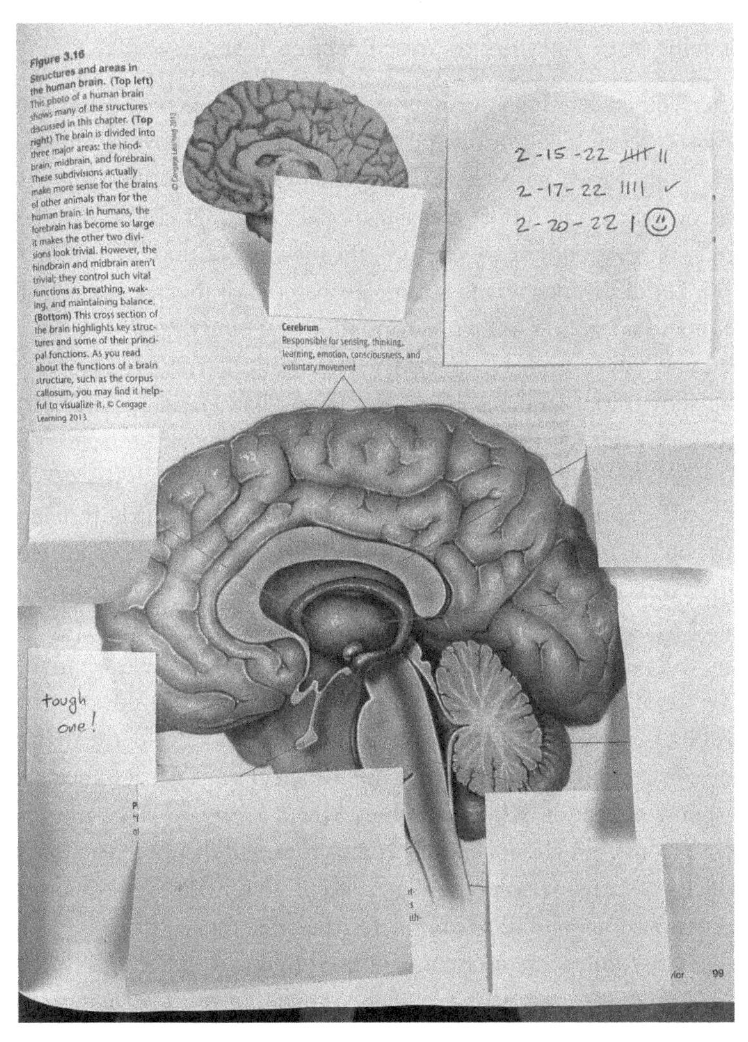

Note. From *Psychology: Themes and Variations* (9th ed, p. 99), by W. Weiten, 2012, Wadsworth Cengage Learning. Copyright 2012 by Wadsworth Cengage Learning.

it correctly) or any other comments to yourself (e.g., highlighting a particularly tough item to learn) on the note itself.

Scoring Your Answers to Your Practice Tests

After you have tested yourself, the next step of successive relearning involves scoring your answer. For instance, while studying complex definitions for an Introductory Chemistry course, you may test yourself on redox and recall "transfer of electrons." Of course, you get credit only if your answer captures the *meaning* of the correct definition. The difficulty with most complex materials is that the first couple of times you try to recall the information you won't get it all correct, and you'll need to check your answer carefully. Even worse, research has shown that students often give themselves credit for incorrect answers, even when the students are highly motivated to score the answers correctly (for a review, see Dunlosky & Lipko, 2007).

The bottom line is that scoring complex answers can be difficult, but you can make it easier. In particular, if you simply recall an answer aloud without writing it down, then you'll need to keep your answer in mind while checking it against the correct answer. For long responses this will be very difficult because you will begin forgetting what you have recalled before you can check your response. To sidestep this problem, we recommend that you write (or type) your response so that you can carefully check it against the correct answer. For instance, the response above for redox has some of the correct ideas (i.e., transfer of electrons), but it is not entirely complete (e.g., a chemical reaction in which one reacting compound gets oxidized, or loses electrons, and the other compound gets reduced, or gains electrons).

After you score an item, you need to decide what to do next. If your answer was incorrect, then you should restudy the correct answer and come back to that item later, to practice retrieving the correct answer. If your response was correct, then you can decide to try it again later or to put it aside to practice it in a different session. Then, you repeat the process until you have correctly recalled all the answers to all the items you decided to practice during that study session. When you are done, you will need to come back to those items again during another session several days later. We recommend you schedule that next practice session right after you finish the first round of practice. If you give each set of items a name (e.g., "Basic Chemistry Concepts"), you can label reminders in a calendar showing when you should return to each set.

The Flash-Cards-Plus Method

There are many variations on the theme of making flash cards as described thus far. We know various apps to help you create flash cards and different widgets, gadgets, and gizmos that you could probably use for retrieval practice. That said, there is something to the act of creating flash cards on index cards. There is one more neat way to modify your flash card use. In the flash-cards-plus method you go beyond having the term on one side and the textbook definition on the other. To help you process the material better, paraphrase the definition in your own words under the textbook one, and then jot down an application of the concept to your own life. Adding these two simple components (your paraphrase and an application) can help increase the depth of your processing of the material and has been shown in classroom research to be effective (Senzaki et al., 2017).

THE POWER OF SUCCESSIVE RELEARNING FOR INTRODUCTORY PSYCHOLOGY

If you try successive relearning, it will be challenging at first because retrieving lengthy answers from memory is much more difficult than reading them. However, the effort will pay off. In fact, if you use this technique for a set of items across three sessions (e.g., spaced 2 or 3 days apart), we can almost guarantee that by the third session you will be easily retrieving many of the responses to the items in the set, even if they are long, complex definitions of science terms—like the ones you need to learn well for almost any introductory course in science.

During one research project, students enrolled in a large introductory course used successive relearning to study some sets of conceptual definitions as described earlier, as well as other definitions they studied any way they liked. For the definitions studied using successive relearning, the students studied small sets of definitions (e.g., eight to 10) at a time, and they worked on each set for four different sessions before their high-stakes exam (Rawson et al., 2013). Two outcomes are noteworthy. First, for the concepts that were learned using successive relearning, the students typically performed about a letter grade and a half better on the high-stakes exam! In addition, the speed with which they recalled the correct answers increased dramatically across the four sessions. Whereas it took more than 30 tries during the first session to correctly recall each of the eight definitions within a set, it took students only about 11 trials to recall them in the fourth session. Put differently, by the fourth successive relearning session most students were correctly recalling each definition on the first attempt or, at worst, on their second try. So, even though learning to recall complex materials will be challenging during an initial session or two, it will eventually be followed by the quick and easy retrieval of even difficult content.

HUDDLE UP

At the beginning of this chapter, we emphasized that retrieval practice works well for two reasons, namely, when you correctly retrieve a question, doing so actually enhances your memory of the retrieved content. In addition, you can use the retrieval attempt to monitor your progress, because when you don't answer a question correctly you know that you need to restudy.

One study method, successive relearning, is a good way to monitor your progress and can help indicate whether you've done enough studying to retain what you need to know for a high-stakes exam. In particular, if you schedule several days between each successive-relearning study session, then how well you perform will give you a pretty good sense about what you will remember. For instance, let's say that you use the technique to study definitions for your Biological Sciences course, and you scheduled four sessions, with 3 days in between each session. Given that you eventually recalled each definition correctly during the first session, if you correctly recalled a definition during the first retrieval attempt in the second session, it means that you retained that information for 3 days. If you correctly recalled the same definition in the third session, then you probably have it down well enough to retain for at least another 3 days, if not much longer. You will retrieve the correct answers more quickly each time you return to them, which will provide even more confidence that you've got it down.

Of course, if you continue to fail to correctly retrieve some information at the beginning of each session, then you have a really great sign that you will not remember the information later; that is, you may find that you keep struggling to remember some definitions. This may indicate that you need to *understand* the material better. So, you may keep forgetting the definition of *redox* because you never understood the meaning of the definition. For pesky material that you just can't seem to memorize, you may need to supplement your studying with other techniques aimed at improving your ability to understand the content. One way to proceed would be to discuss the material with a fellow student or your instructor. Other possibilities involve changing the technique you use to study the to-be-learned material. We discuss some of those techniques—such as self-explanation, imagery, and so on—in other chapters.

Key Training Tips

- Practice retrieval of the same content across multiple study sessions.
- Stick Your Landing by scheduling two or more weekly study sessions for each class, and correctly retrieve the answers of course material during each session.

Go for the Gold With an Advanced Reading

Rawson, K. A., & Dunlosky, J. (in press). Successive relearning: An under-explored but potent technique for obtaining and maintaining knowledge. *Current Directions in Psychological Science.*

Drawing by Paige Herrboldt. Printed with permission.

CHAPTER 6

SPECIALTY STRATEGIES FOR PROBLEM-SOLVING COURSES: INTERLEAVED PRACTICE, SELF-EXPLANATION, AND WORKED EXAMPLES

In this chapter, you will learn

- why mixing problems can help you learn how to solve difficult problems,
- why talking to yourself about what you are learning can boost your understanding, and
- why studying worked-out solutions to problems is a great way to begin problem solving.

Stephanie has been using a variety of the learning strategies in her arsenal to prepare for her first exam in Introductory Psychology. She definitely is a Spacer (see Chapter 4) and has scheduled several 2-hour study sessions a week to study for this course. During each session, she has diligently used successive relearning to master the definitions relevant to the most important concepts in the chapters assigned for the exam. Stephanie has learned these concepts well, but she runs into difficulty when she attempts to solve problems from those chapters, such as computing probabilities for the introductory chapter on statistics and for solving problems about classical and operant conditioning. She needs help to move forward with success: It's not that the strategies she is using to learn how to solve these problems are letting her down, but those strategies just cannot solve all of her difficulties while learning and comprehending the material. What is Stephanie to do now?

Let's begin by looking backward: In the preceding chapters, we introduced strategies that can improve your achievement in mastering a broad range of materials and learning objectives. Retrieval practice is an excellent example of a broadly effective strategy because it can be used to help you learn a wide range of materials and prepare for many different kinds of exams. In the world of carpentry, retrieval practice would be analogous to a hammer that you can use to accomplish many different tasks. Sometimes, however, you may need a specialty strategy—not a hammer to pound away at content with but a tool that can help you progress on more detailed projects, like using sandpaper to smooth out rough edges.

Such tools are critical, and in this chapter we introduce several specialty strategies: interleaved practice, self-explanation, and using worked examples. These strategies are listed in Table 6.1, and in the

TABLE 6.1. Three Specialty Strategies to Use While You Are Studying and Learning to Solve Problems

Strategy	Brief definition	Example application
Interleaved practice	Mixing practice of different kinds of concepts	Solving problems
Self-explanation	Explaining something to yourself	Learning how a process works
Worked examples	Studying an example of how a problem is solved	Solving problems

next three sections we separately discuss details about the strategy and why it may improve learning, evidence that the strategy works from the laboratory and the classroom, and tips on how to get the most out of each strategy. In the final section, we encourage you to really study like a champion by combining these strategies with each other and with the all-purpose strategies described elsewhere in this book.

INTERLEAVED PRACTICE

The first specialized strategy to look at is known as *interleaved practice*. The goal of interleaved practice (also called *interleaving*) is to mix up your studying with different kinds of concepts or problems. The best way to illustrate this strategy—and probably one of the best applications for it—involves solving math problems. Students typically use *blocked practice* in this situation, not interleaved practice. Imagine that you are learning to solve problems related to the volumes of different solids in a geometry class, such as the ones pictured in Figure 6.1. In a traditional classroom, you may first learn about the formula to solve for the volume of the wedge (top right panel) and then practice solving many problems of this type (i.e., solving for the volume of different-sized wedges) in a block. So, you may solve eight or 10 of these wedge problems until you decide you are comfortable with them. Then, you move on to the formula for a different solid, such as the spheroid (top left panel). As before, you'd practice solving many problems involving spheroids in a large block. In this example, while learning to solve problems for any one kind of problem (e.g., a wedge, a spheroid, half-cone), you are blocking the practice for each problem.

> *For interleaved practice, the goal is to mix up your studying with different kinds of concepts or problems.*

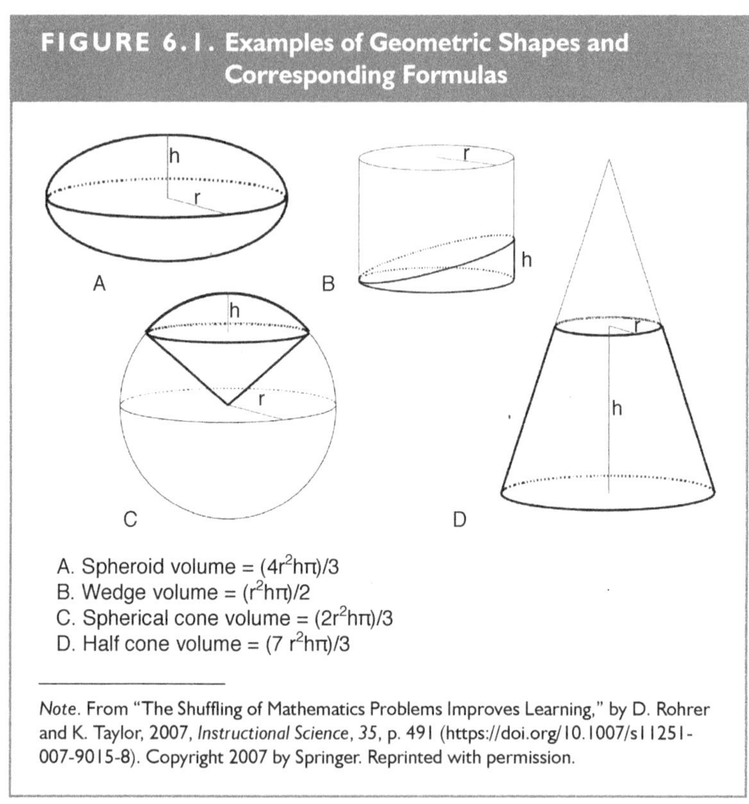

FIGURE 6.1. Examples of Geometric Shapes and Corresponding Formulas

Note. From "The Shuffling of Mathematics Problems Improves Learning," by D. Rohrer and K. Taylor, 2007, *Instructional Science*, *35*, p. 491 (https://doi.org/10.1007/s11251-007-9015-8). Copyright 2007 by Springer. Reprinted with permission.

In contrast to blocked practice, interleaving involves first studying the formulas for all of the kinds of problems (e.g., all those presented in Figure 6.1) and then randomly choosing a kind of problem to solve. In this case, you might first solve a wedge problem, then a cylinder problem, followed by a spheroid problem, and you'd continue this pattern until you can accurately solve all of the kinds of problems. This is similar to learning to a criterion (see Chapter 5), but for interleaving you continue to practice all the problems (in a random order) until you understand how to solve each one and can do so with consistency. Most important, in contrast to blocked practice, interleaved practice can improve your learning and memory for how to solve problems.

What's the Evidence for the Benefit of Using Interleaved Practice?

The relative power of interleaving versus blocking practice has been explored extensively, with many different learning materials, and in both the laboratory and the classroom. This kind of research is typically tested with what cognitive scientists call *near transfer*. This simply means that what you are practicing is not exactly how you get tested; that is, you must transfer what you learned while studying to perform correctly. For instance, in regard to Figure 6.1, involving volumes, you may practice solving a volume of a spheroid with a radius (r) of 2 inches and a height (h) of 4 inches, but then during the final test you would be asked to calculate the volume of a spheroid with a difference radius and height, say of 3.5 and 10 inches, respectively. If you were learning the painting styles of different artists, you may study specific paintings by five different artists, and then on the final test you would be asked to indicate which artist is responsible for each painting. If new paintings are shown during the test, then the test would involve transfer. Studying to perform well on tests that involve transfer of knowledge is exactly what most students want to do because tests are rarely administered in exactly the way you practice studying (even when your practice involves self-testing, as we recommended in Chapter 5, often you would not be retrieving the identical answers that you will be tested on during a high-stakes exam).

Final performance on transfer tests (tests involving different versions of each problem) is often substantially better for students who chose interleaved practice over blocked practice to study. The benefits of using interleaved practice to learn math are perhaps the most well documented and impressive, so consider an outcome from one investigation involving an authentic education context (Rohrer et al., 2020). Over 4 months, seventh-grade students from more than 50 classes solved math problems relating to different concepts they were learning in class, such as solving inequality equations and simplifying algebraic equations. A worksheet presented either mixed problems across the different concepts (interleaved practice) or included problems from one concept (blocked practice). One month after a final review of the concepts, the students received a final test, which included new problems for each concept. Their final performance demonstrated a substantial benefit of interleaved practice, with students who had used interleaved practice performing 23% better than those who had used blocked practice.

Why does interleaving boost students' learning and performance? It turns out that the power of interleaving resides in several factors, and understanding these factors is critical to reaping the full benefits of this strategy. You are already well acquainted with the first factor, *spaced practice*. Blocking practice involves massing all the practice for one kind of problem at the same time, whereas interleaving by necessity involves spaced practice. Consider our example about calculating the volume of different solids. With an interleaved schedule, you might first solve a wedge problem, and then you would interleave by solving problems for the other three solids (spheroid, spherical cone, half cone), and only after you finished the others would you go back to solve another wedge problem. So, the practice for each kind of problem would be spaced in time, and we know that spaced practice typically leads to much better learning (for details, see Chapter 4).

The second factor—*discriminative contrast*—is unique to interleaved practice. Note that by interleaving practice across different kinds of problems you would be better able to contrast (or compare) one kind of problem with another because they would be practiced one right after another. In some classes, being able to identify the type of problem you are trying to solve is an important part of the exam. For instance, if you can identify what kind of problem you are trying to solve, you will have an easier time deciding which formula to use. The best way to practice this skill would be to interleave types of problems at random, so you do not know what kind you are facing ahead of time. The challenge in obtaining this benefit of interleaving is that you need to be given the to-be-solved problems so that your first task is to identify the specific type of problem you are solving. Unfortunately, textbooks often present practice problems in a massed fashion so that when you begin to practice you know ahead of time that you are trying to solve problems that focus on classical conditioning or operant conditioning (e.g., if the chapter is on "Learning" in Introductory Psychology), so you would not get practice identifying the type of problem. Instead, those problems need to be interleaved and presented in such a way that you would have to practice identifying the kind of problem you must solve.

Tips for Using Interleaved Practice

We recommend you interleave your practice whenever you can, in part because doing so takes advantage of a technique (i.e., spaced practice) that we are sure will benefit your learning. A challenge will be that practice problems are often presented in a massed fashion, such as when multiple versions of one kind of problem are presented at the end of a chapter. We recommend, if possible, gathering examples from all chapters and mixing them up before practicing. Although this makes practice a bit more difficult, it is a more effective use of your time. The struggle is worth it, though, because mixing up your practice by interleaving can help you learn.

> *Often, textbooks will present multiple examples of the same type of problem at the end of a chapter. We recommend gathering examples from all chapters and mixing them up before practicing.*

Sometimes a sufficient number of practice problems is not available to allow you to easily interleave problems of different kinds. Your instructor may not provide any problems other than those presented during lectures, and your textbook may not provide enough. One solution would be to form a study group in your class, with each member of the group assigned to develop a few practice problems of each kind you need to learn. You can then swap questions or take turns solving them, as long as you make sure to mix all the problems (across different kinds) before beginning.

SELF-EXPLANATION

Self-explanation involves generating an explanation for why a particular fact, concept, or way to solve a problem is correct. You can use it whenever you are studying. It first involves asking yourself "why," "what," or "how?" For instance, if you are reading a chapter about perception, you may ask yourself, "What exactly is perception?" or "How is perception different from sensation?" Another example involves learning statistics; when you are studying a worked example that solves a statistics problem (e.g., how to compute a standard error for a mean), you may ask yourself, "Why is that particular step of the solution necessary?" Of course, after you pose a question, the next step is to provide an answer: a self-explanation. It really is just that simple, but let's dive a bit deeper into the evidence and how you might use self-explanation while studying.

What's the Evidence for the Benefit of Using Self-Explanation?

Before we turn to the evidence, we want to acknowledge that learning to solve problems can be challenging. It is also something you will be doing in many courses, including computer science, chemistry, cognitive psychology, mathematics, and so on. Of course, solving problems can be fun as well, and to illustrate, please take a moment to solve the logic problem in Figure 6.2 (which is based on the classic Wason Selection Task). Each card in this figure has a musical instrument on one side and a number on the other side. For this problem, you need to identify which cards need to be turned over to evaluate the correctness of the following rule: If a card has a guitar on one side, it has a 9 on the other side.

Did you try to solve it? The answer is that you would turn over the first two cards only, although many people say that the card with 9 on it should also be turned over (but if something other than a guitar is on the back of the 9 card, that doesn't mean all guitar cards do not

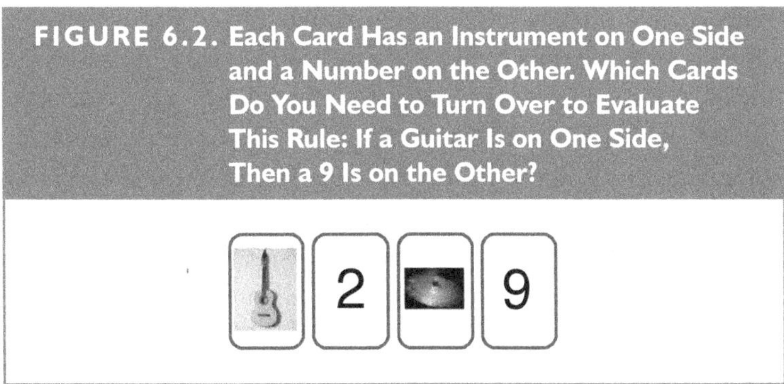

FIGURE 6.2. Each Card Has an Instrument on One Side and a Number on the Other. Which Cards Do You Need to Turn Over to Evaluate This Rule: If a Guitar Is on One Side, Then a 9 Is on the Other?

have a 9 on the other side, so turning this card over provides no evidence). Solving these problems involves understanding how to apply the rules of logic, and, as with learning how to solve many different kinds of problems, these can be difficult to understand and master.

Berry (1983) conducted one of the first investigations of self-explanation. In the study, students were given brief instructions on how to solve logic problems like the Wason Selection Task (Figure 6.2). After receiving instructions, students were able to practice solving this task. Some students were asked to explain the reasons why they chose (or did not choose) each card; that is, a student may ask, "Why did I choose the card with a 9 on it?" Other students just practiced solving the problems. During practice, all students did well, answering over 90% of the problems correctly. More important, the students were later asked to solve abstract versions of the logic problems, which would require a deeper understanding of logic. For students who self-explained during practice, their performance on the abstract versions was still close to 90% correct, whereas those who did not self-explain during practice answered fewer than 30% of the abstract problems correctly.

Why might self-explanation improve your understanding of material? Although research is not available to firmly demonstrate why self-explanation works, a few prevailing theories are available. First, when you try to explain something, one way to do so is to combine information you already know with what you are trying to learn. So, students who explained each card during practice may have reflected more on the instructions on how to solve the problems (something they had just learned) and how to use these instructions while solving other problems. Second, you could easily practice solving problems in a relatively unengaged manner, such as by making a quick educated guess so as to get feedback about the correct answer. In Figure 6.2, you may choose the first and final card simply because they have objects (a guitar and a 9) on them that appear in the target rule (if guitar on one side, then 9 on other side). Self-explaining would naturally slow you down and hence may encourage you to consider the options more deeply and push you to evaluate whether they are correct.

Finally, as noted earlier, we suspect that self-explanation can benefit your performance by helping you to monitor your performance more accurately. Imagine that you are in a biology course, and you are trying to understand all the processes involved in photosynthesis. You have your textbook open, but instead of merely rereading the material you decide to try out self-explanation and attempt to explain each step in the process to yourself. If you can explain each process correctly, then you are probably in good shape, especially if you are explaining the processes by retrieving them from memory (see Chapter 4). In contrast, if you cannot explain some or all of the processes to yourself, then you have identified content for which you may need some further instruction. Perhaps you could read a different summary of the processes, ask another student for guidance, or even get help from your instructor.

Tips for Using Self-Explanation

People naturally like to explain themselves—just ask friends to explain anything they are doing (why they ordered a particular meal at a restaurant, why they want to see a particular movie that evening, etc.), and we suspect your friends would never say, "I don't know." Instead, an explanation—sometimes detailed—would be provided for the reasons behind their decisions and preferences. Almost everyone loves to explain themselves, and we recommend that you direct your natural propensity to explain toward your studying. Admittedly, so far not much research has focused on exploring the best ways to explain or the best times to explain, so our recommendations here are based more on our informed intuitions as teachers and as (former) students.

We suspect that self-explanation will pay off the most when you already have a head start with the target material; that is, you'll be able to use self-explanation most effectively after you have been introduced to the material. Even in the investigation by Berry (1983) described above, the students were first instructed how to solve the logic problems before they began practicing and explaining their choices. In fact, if you have no background knowledge in a domain we suspect that self-explanation would largely be a waste of time, simply because you would have nowhere to begin. With this in mind, a great time to start using this strategy would be when you first begin reviewing material. For instance, you are exposed to material when you are taking notes in a class, so later that day, when you sit down to first review your notes, consider trying to explain any of the content that affords explanation to yourself (e.g., memorizing the labels for brain parts would not require explanation, but how the blood–brain barrier keeps toxins from attacking your brain would). By using this strategy when you first review your notes you would not only be engaging the material more deeply than if you were merely reading it, but you also would be able to immediately evaluate whether you do, in fact, understand the material.

The following are some questions you can ask yourself as you self-explain. Some can be used while you are reading your textbook or notes, and others can be used when you are practicing solving problems.

When reading textbooks or your notes:

- How does this process (e.g., photosynthesis) work, and why?
- What is a good example to illustrate this particular concept?
- Why is the example provided in the text an appropriate example for the concept it illustrates?
- Why does the author say that "such-and-such" (almost anything can go here) is true?

When solving any kind of problem:

- Before beginning, ask yourself, what kind of problem is this, and what are possible solutions?
- Have I solved a problem like this before, and how do I go about solving it?
- Why is a particular step in a problem solution the correct (or incorrect) one?
- Why do I seem to be having difficulties understanding this problem?

Asking such questions will be much more engaging than simply reading a text or going through the motions of applying a problem solution, and this engagement will itself produce challenges (e.g., when you cannot answer a question) that can slow you down, prompting deeper understanding of the content.

Most important, remember that the goal of self-explanation is not to "explain" only when you are sure that you can easily generate a correct explanation. You should instead challenge yourself with the questions you are unsure about because failing to explain a concept correctly allows you to monitor your understanding and thereby can provide an important stepping-stone toward eventual mastery of any material. In such cases, consider reviewing your material to identify the answers to your questions and, when in doubt, consider seeking help from other students in class or your instructor.

WORKED EXAMPLES

Solving problems in unfamiliar domains can be challenging, but often it is necessary to excel in some courses, such as mathematics, physics, or chemistry. In general, problem solving involves three stages: (a) representing the problem (i.e., identifying what kind of problem it is and how to go about solving it), (b) generating solutions to a problem, and (c) evaluating the quality of the answers to the problem. One way to help you solve novel problems is to study *worked examples*, which provide all the steps in a solution for a particular problem as well as the answer to the problem. Using worked examples largely focuses on the second stage: generating and implementing the steps to a solution, but we now briefly consider each step before diving into the power of worked examples. (If you are already familiar with the basics of representing a problem and how to evaluate the quality of your solutions, please move on to the discussion of worked examples.)

Representing a problem correctly sometimes is the most difficult step of solving problems, especially tricky ones. Before you read on, try to solve the nine-dot problem presented in Figure 6.3. Many people struggle to solve this, even though the solution itself turns out to be simple (well, at least *after* you know the solution). People struggle because they often begin by representing the problem in a way that makes it impossible to solve: Most people assume that all

FIGURE 6.3. The Nine-Dot Problem

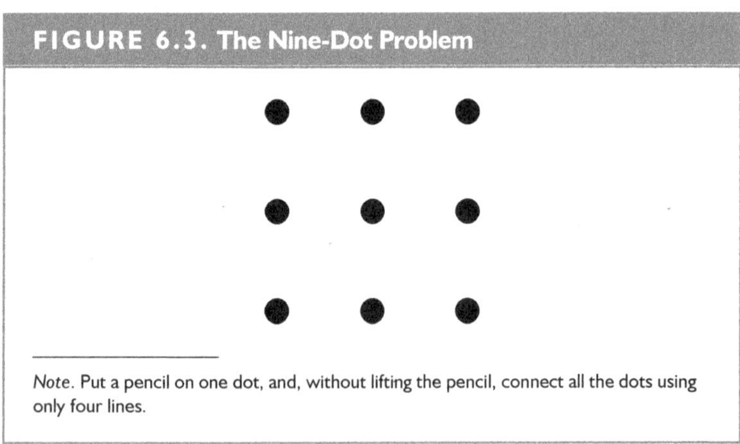

Note. Put a pencil on one dot, and, without lifting the pencil, connect all the dots using only four lines.

four lines must stay within the boundary produced by the eight outer dots. However, the four lines can—and must—extend beyond those borders, and when people represent the problem correctly a solution is typically close at hand (for the solution, see Figure 6.4). Thus, representing a problem accurately involves understanding the possible solutions to a problem (e.g., that the lines can extend beyond the borders), but doing so may also require you to classify a problem correctly. The importance of such classification is perhaps most obvious in courses like physics, engineering, and chemistry. In physics, you may have an exam with 10 problems to solve, and you must first correctly classify a problem—is it a problem about force, velocity, or friction?—to be able to choose an appropriate solution. As noted earlier, using interleaved schedules for solving problems will give you a chance to practice identifying each type of problem.

Even when you represent a problem correctly, this does not mean you will be able to solve it. So, you may correctly identify a problem as one that involves determining the velocity of a constantly accelerating object at a certain point in time, yet, if you do not know the correct solutions and how to use them (in this case, a series of equations), then you will struggle. In this case you would need to be able to recall all the equations accurately (which is a great chore for successive relearning) and understand how to use them. Understanding how to solve a problem can be rather difficult and may be one reason why all students don't major in physics or engineering. Even so, many courses require solving problems, and using worked examples (as we describe further shortly) should become a go-to strategy when you have difficulties understanding how to solve them.

> *One benefit of self-explanation is that it allows you to discover what you don't yet understand.*

FIGURE 6.4. Solution to the Nine-Dot Problem

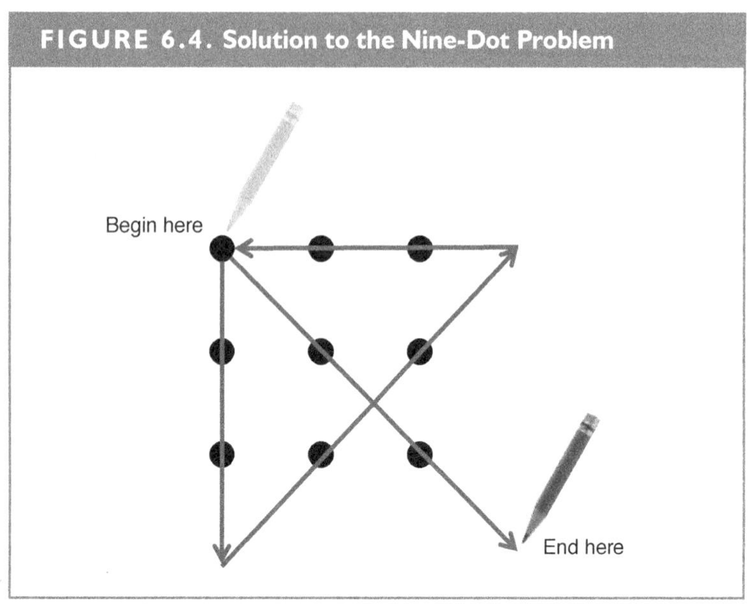

The final step is evaluating the quality of your answer and solution; that is, did you respond with the correct answer, and whether you did or not, did you choose the correct solution? Skipping this step can certainly lead to errors: When John uses the nine-dot problem in his lecture on problem solving, some students hand in the problem as "solved correctly" when in fact they used five (one too many) lines. I'm sure these students can count to 5, so they just didn't carefully check their answer. One recommendation here would be to remember to always check your answer, and for complicated problems (as in physics or engineering), when you do not have the correct answer you should evaluate whether you chose the correct solution but computed the wrong answer or whether the solution you chose was incorrect. If you were incorrect because you chose an incorrect solution, then you need to diagnose why you did so. Is it because you are confusing different kinds of problems (in which case some interleaved practice may be useful) or because you had little understanding of which solution to use (in which case you may need to revisit your textbook or notes)? Also, it's important to note that checking the quality of your answers pertains to your self-explanations as well—whenever you are asking and answering "why" or "what" questions to yourself, if you have any doubt about whether your answer is correct then it's time to look it up or ask an instructor or another student to help out. In fact, we suspect that one benefit of self-explanation is that it allows you to monitor and discover what you don't yet understand, so make sure you check the quality of your own self-explanations!

Worked examples can be super useful when you are struggling with the solution stage of problem solving. A worked example is simply that: It provides a detailed example of how to solve a problem. Worked examples can be rather complicated because solutions to challenging problems are often complex. When instructors discuss how to solve problems during a course lecture they often walk students through the steps of how to solve an example problem. They are, in essence, giving you a worked example. Absolutely make sure you jot these worked examples in your notes, including all the steps in a solution and the reasons for them. Then, when you are practicing solving new problems, if you get stuck, revisit and study your worked example. Your goal is to figure out which steps you are not implementing correctly (or forgetting) so that you will have more success solving the next problem. In fact, you may not even want to wait until you struggle: Some research indicates that beginning by studying worked examples—especially when you are a novice and just beginning to learn a new domain—and then moving to solving problems increases the speed with which students learn to solve challenging problems (for a review, see van Gog et al., 2019).

What's the Evidence for the Benefit of Studying Worked Examples?

The bulk of the evidence that establishes the power of using worked examples has come from research conducted in laboratories, often using complex problems (e.g., how to write a computer program) with novice students. We now describe one such experiment, which generally captures the approach used to evaluate the efficacy of worked examples and includes some of the most impressive outcomes from this literature.

Paas and van Merrienboer (1994) provided some initial instruction to students in a trade school on the geometry principles needed to operate computer numerically controlled machinery. After the students had been given the instructions for how to solve these complex problems, six problems were presented for practice. Some students received conventional practice, attempting to solve a practice problem and then receiving feedback about their answer. Students in the worked-example group only studied the worked example for each problem. After practice, students then had to solve new problems of the same type. The students who had practiced solving problems took more than twice as much time to solve the new problems than did the students who had studied worked-example problems. Also, despite using half as much time during practice, the scores of the students who had studied worked examples were about twice as high compared with those of the students who had solved problems during practice.

The reason why studying worked examples was more helpful than solving problems in this case is pretty straightforward. The students had little background knowledge—or a deeper understanding of the structure of the solutions—of how these problems should be solved to begin with, so trying to solve a problem that one cannot represent properly or cannot generate reasonable solutions to would be a relatively inefficient use of time. In such cases, the worked examples allow students to develop a bird's-eye view of the schema for the problem, including the ultimate goal and the solution needed to obtain it. It is important to note that after you use worked examples to learn how to solve problems, you should shift from studying worked examples to actually solving them from scratch. In other words, after you have a better understanding of the schema, then worked examples are no longer needed because you know enough to gain further knowledge by attempting to solve new problems. In contrast to novices, experts sometimes are hindered by worked examples and are better off spending their practice time trying to solve new problems. So, when you are starting out in a new area that involves problem solving, you may want to begin by studying how others have successfully solved the problem; it could give you a good head start toward understanding a problem and how to accurately solve it.

Tips for Using Worked Examples

When looking at a worked example, perhaps ask yourself, "What are all the steps in the solution, and why is each step relevant to solving the problem?" In essence, this combines the strategy of worked problems with that of self-explanation, and combining effective strategies is often a great idea (see Chapter 8). After you feel comfortable with the worked example, try solving a new problem from the beginning. If you continue to struggle, you should study the worked example for the new problem, if it is available, and then move on to another new problem. If you are still struggling, then you may want to use a *faded worked example*. For faded examples, you would study steps for the first half of the problem and then solve the remaining portion. When you do that correctly, you then fade (or withdraw) more of the worked example for the next problem; for instance, you may study the first quarter of the worked example and then try to solve the remainder. Thus, you would need to correctly solve more of it yourself the next time. At some point, you won't need any example to succeed.

The study we just described illustrates learning to solve a problem of a particular kind, such as one kind of statistics problem or one kind of chemistry problem. Studying worked examples is meant to help you develop a deeper understanding of the second stage of problem solving. However, even when you have met that goal for a particular kind of problem, remember that on an exam (or in the real world) the first thing you may need to do is to identify the problem and represent it correctly (the first stage of problem solving). Because different kinds of problems within a domain often look like the same problem to novices, you still may perform poorly on an exam if you cannot accurately identify each problem even if you can solve each problem *after* you know what kind of problem it is. If you are struggling with identification, then it is time to set up a study session in which you use the interleaving technique, which forces you to identify problem types before you begin solving.

HUDDLE UP

In this chapter, we have described three strategies—interleaved practice, self-explaining, and using worked examples—that are aimed at improving your ability to understand and comprehend conceptually difficult material and solve problems of all kinds. We encourage you to try them all, but to really harness the power of these and other strategies introduced in this book you will need to combine the strategies for particular situations. The strategies can be combined in numerous ways, and part of being a Study Champion involves choosing to use an additional strategy when your go-to strategies are faltering. Given how many strategies are available, the number of combinations is rather daunting, so in Chapter 8 we provide examples of some potent combinations.

The various strategies introduced in this chapter and earlier ones can be used more generally to learn how to solve problems from many different courses, such as chemistry, physics, engineering, mathematics, and so forth. So, when you are studying, consider your current learning goal, and choose the best strategy for the job. To help out, we have listed the strategies in Figure 6.5, along with how you might harness them to bolster your performance in classes that involve problem solving. For instance, in regard to Figure 6.5, if you are having difficulties understanding why, and in what order, you should be applying solutions to a difficult problem in a math class, then you may want to study a worked example of that problem. In this case, you may further improve your ability to solve the problem on exams by explaining why each step of the solution is essential to correctly solving the problem. So, consider referring back to this figure when needed to identify which strategies may be most useful, and then perhaps revisit the more detailed instructions about that strategy in the text. We hope this guidance gives you a bird's-eye view on when you might use each strategy to study like a champion.

Key Training Tips

- Try to explain difficult concepts to yourself; this is a valuable approach to studying.
- Stick Your Landing by knowing when to supplement your studying with these strategies: Use interleaving to study

FIGURE 6.5. Study Strategies for Problem-Solving Courses

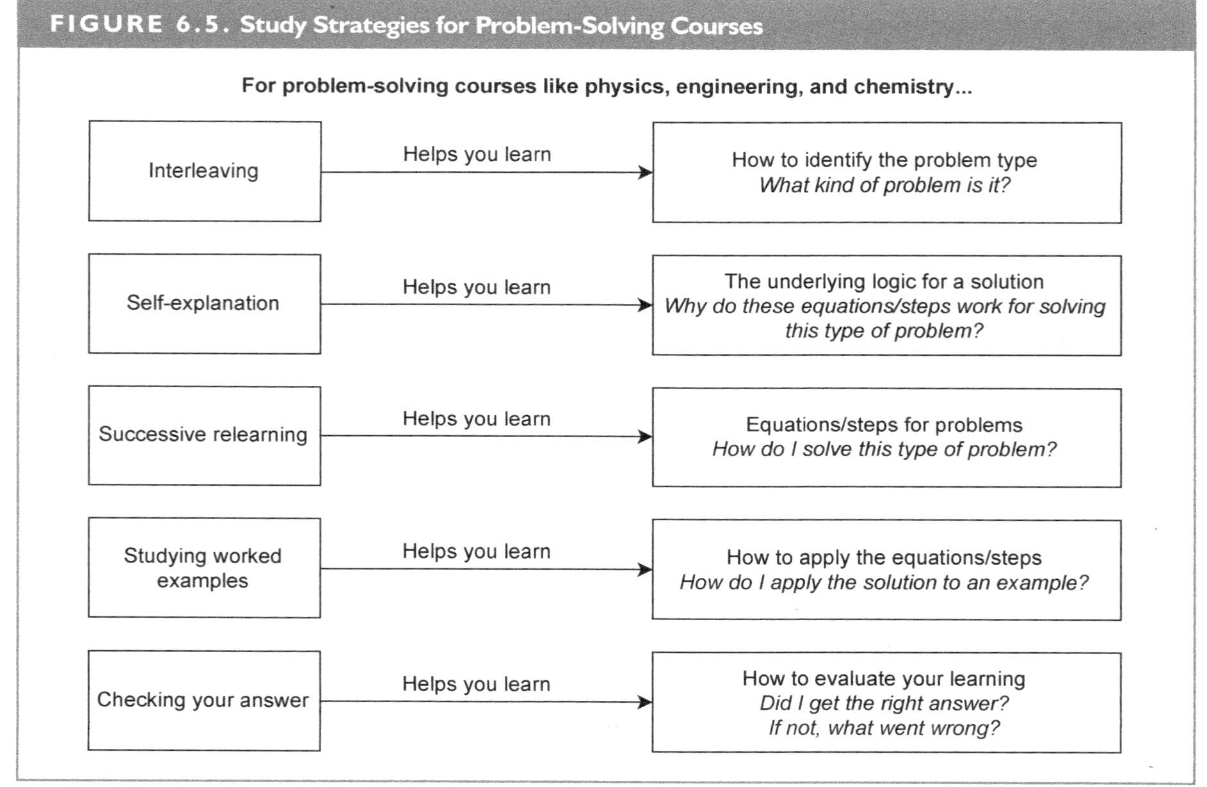
For problem-solving courses like physics, engineering, and chemistry...
Interleaving
Helps you learn
How to identify the problem type
What kind of problem is it?
Self-explanation
Helps you learn
The underlying logic for a solution
Why do these equations/steps work for solving this type of problem?
Successive relearning
Helps you learn
Equations/steps for problems
How do I solve this type of problem?
Studying worked examples
Helps you learn
How to apply the equations/steps
How do I apply the solution to an example?
Checking your answer
Helps you learn
How to evaluate your learning
Did I get the right answer?
If not, what went wrong?

concepts and problems that you confuse with one another, try out self-explanation when you are studying your notes, and study worked examples when you are beginning to learn to solve new kinds of problems.

Go for the Gold With an Advanced Reading

Dehaene, S. (2021). *How we learn: The new science of education and the brain*. Penguin.

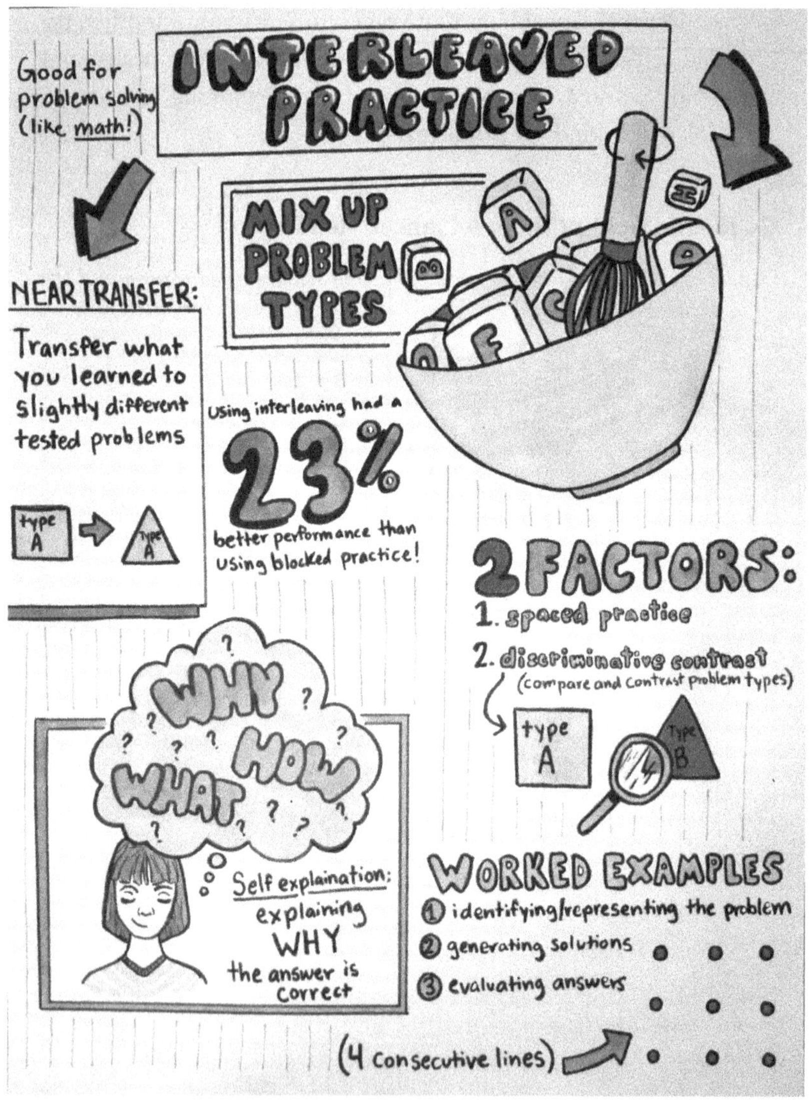

Drawing by Paige Herrboldt. Printed with permission.

CHAPTER 7

WHEN TO USE HIGHLIGHTING, REREADING, SUMMARIZING, AND IMAGERY

In this chapter, you will learn

- when to use highlighters to prepare for further study sessions,
- when to reread and summarize material to propel your studying success, and
- why developing mental images may help you retain some course content.

We talk to a lot of students about how they study and what they believe works best, and we are pretty sure that many students are already using some of the most effective strategies, such as taking notes the right way and using retrieval practice. We hope that you are already using at least some of them, and for those of you who aren't, we encourage you to try out the recommendations we have offered in the preceding chapters, such as planning and scheduling when you will study for each course, managing your time, using successive relearning, and so forth. Nevertheless, we are not suggesting that you abandon all the other strategies you have been using. Some of them may not necessarily be the most effective, but when used correctly and in combination with other strategies, they make great additions to your strategy toolbox. We consider four of these strategies in this chapter: (a) highlighting, (b) rereading, (c) summarizing, and (d) imagery.

Before we discuss how to use each one, consider why these strategies are not generally considered as effective as those we've already introduced. One criterion used to evaluate the effectiveness of a strategy is whether using it improves students' retention and comprehension of what they are studying (e.g., Dunlosky et al., 2013). For instance, imagine two groups of students reading a chapter while studying for an exam: One group reads the chapter, whereas the other students use a highlighter to try to underscore the most important content while they are reading. All of the students are given the same amount of time to study and then are tested over the content. It turns out that performance on the test would likely not be meaningfully different for the two groups of students; that is, highlighting may provide a small boost to your learning while you read, but it is not an effective strategy for mastering the content. Likewise, occasionally rereading notes or the textbook (vs. doing nothing) has little impact on students' learning.

These strategies are not entirely without merit. When used in combination with other strategies, they can help you along the way to reaching your learning goals. We suspect that most students understand that highlighting itself does not improve their learning that much (that's not why you highlight, right?) but would be disappointed to find out that rereading can be so ineffective. So, with this warning in mind, let's turn to how you can use these strategies while you are studying like a champion.

HIGHLIGHTING

Open up almost any used book at your university bookstore, and you'll see a collage of colors and underlines, like a rainbow threw up all over the pages. This is even true despite the fact that most textbooks come pre-highlighted, with all the most important content in bold, italics, or offset in the margin. Still, most of us highlight, even though it may not be the most effective studying strategy. In fact, one of the authors of this book is quick to note that he has a favorite highlighter that he lets no one—absolutely no one—borrow. So, what is our attraction to highlighting? Sometimes highlighting can help us remember a bit more of what we are reading than we would remember without highlighting, maybe it helps some of us to stop our minds from wandering, and maybe some of us are just attracted to those bright bold colors (and occasionally scents) of our favorite highlighters. Even so, highlighting will not produce mastery and likely won't turn a C grade into an A. How can you use such a simple and well-loved implement to enhance your achievement?

The highlighter is a tool that can launch your studying—it is the beginning of the journey and not an end in itself. As we noted earlier, although reading a section of a textbook and then going back to highlight it afterward may actually help you to process the text a bit better (for a review, see Miyatsu et al., 2018), using highlighting as your sole study strategy will not allow you to master the material enough to excel on your exams. Thus, our most important recommendation is to highlight with specific goals in mind. One key goal is to use the highlighter as a way to prepare for a more effective learning strategy. For instance, you could highlight the content that you want to study using successive relearning. After you highlight the key content, you would then return to it to either make flash cards (for use in self-testing) or perhaps use the sticky-note technique (described in Chapter 5) to prepare the highlighted content for retrieval practice. As mentioned, many textbooks already have the most important material identified in some manner, so you may just want to highlight the material that the instructor has emphasized.

Another application is to highlight the content that you do not fully understand as you are going through your first reading.

That way, you can return to this content later, to try to understand it better, such as reviewing the same content from a different author (e.g., if you don't understand photosynthesis in your textbook, perhaps someone else will explain it better for you) or seeking help from a fellow student or an instructor (for tips on seeking help, see Chapter 9). Here is where a rainbow of colors may come in handy for highlighting like a champion: One color can be used to indicate what you're confused about, whereas another can indicate material that should be prepared for further learning (e.g., for flash cards). These are just two goals to consider as you are highlighting, and no doubt you may develop others as well. The important point is that highlighting isn't the end of your learning journey but instead is a tool to help you begin—so, do use your highlighters, but do so with purpose.

REREADING

Between class notes, textbooks, worksheets, and more, a lot of class material often needs to be read. If the course material that you need to learn is written in words, then you will need to read, whether that happens to be notes from your class, textbook materials, worksheets from your instructors, and so on. If you forgot what you read or did not understand it, then it makes sense that you'll need to go back to read that material again. But if you do go back to reread the material, will that increase the chances you understand and remember it?

To answer these questions, consider some outcomes from an investigation conducted by Rawson and Kintsch (2005), who had college students read a challenging *Scientific American* article on carbon sequestration. Some students read the text one time, and other students read it twice. For those who reread it, some reread it immediately after they finished the initial reading (called *massed study*), and some of them reread it a week later (*spaced study*). The latter group was using a spaced-study schedule, but instead of studying with retrieval practice (as discussed in Chapter 5), they were merely rereading. Half of the students in each of the three groups (single reading, massed rereading, and spaced rereading) took a test immediately after they finished reading the article the first time; the other half of the students in each of the groups took that test 2 days after reading (either after the first reading, for the single-reading group, or after the second reading, for the rereading groups). The latter 2-day retention interval is important because it most closely reflects studying the night before an exam. Finally, the test involved short-answer questions that measured how well the students understood carbon sequestration.

The results are presented in Figure 7.1, and several outcomes are noteworthy. Consider performance on the immediate test (left panel of the figure): In this case, rereading was better than a single reading, and massed rereading was just as good (if not a bit better) than spaced rereading. However, you are rarely tested immediately after studying, and often your learning goal is to retain your understanding of the most important content over longer periods of time. Thus, outcomes for the delayed test (right panel of Figure 7.1) are arguably more relevant. For the delayed test, performance was not much better for those who massed their rereading than for those who just read the text once; rereading just did not have a long-term impact. By contrast, those who spaced their rereading retained much more of what they had initially learned from the article across the 2 days; that is, performance for the spaced-study group was about the same whether they were tested immediately after studying versus when they were tested after a 2-day delay. Most important, this group outperformed the other two on the delayed test. In summary, rereading your textbook and notes can improve your retention, and rereading likely will have the largest impact when you space it across time.

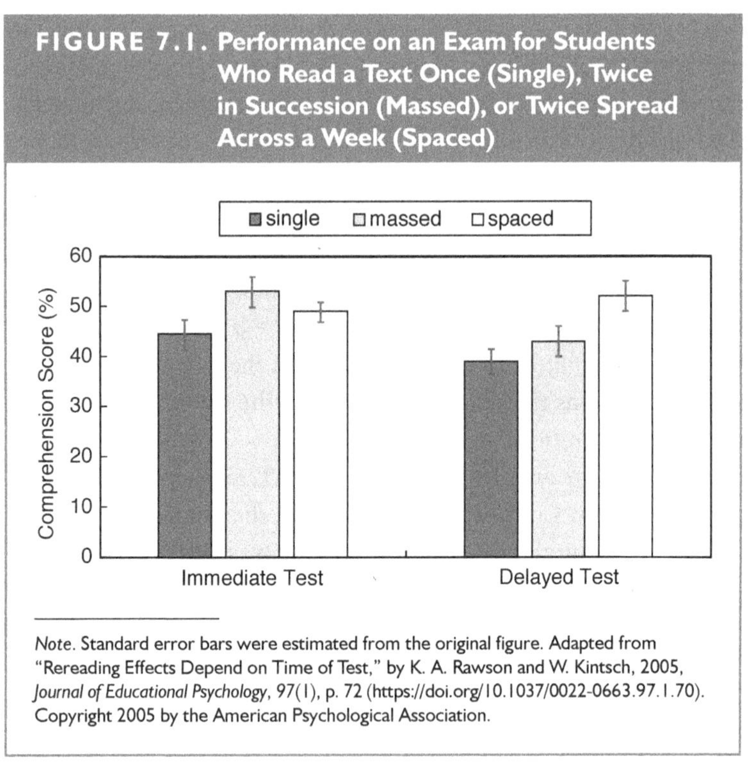

FIGURE 7.1. Performance on an Exam for Students Who Read a Text Once (Single), Twice in Succession (Massed), or Twice Spread Across a Week (Spaced)

Note. Standard error bars were estimated from the original figure. Adapted from "Rereading Effects Depend on Time of Test," by K. A. Rawson and W. Kintsch, 2005, *Journal of Educational Psychology*, 97(1), p. 72 (https://doi.org/10.1037/0022-0663.97.1.70). Copyright 2005 by the American Psychological Association.

Another aspect of these outcomes is also noteworthy but is often missed by educational researchers: Even though the spaced-study group had the best performance at the 2-day delay, the level of performance that the students achieved was only a bit above 50%. Thus, if this were a high-stakes exam in an authentic classroom, the spaced-study group still would have failed. In this case, perhaps if those students would go back a few more times to read the content yet again across different sessions spaced by multiple days, they would eventually achieve a passing grade. But, as we discussed in Chapter 5, an even better approach would be to use retrieval practice during those spaced sessions and then revisit the content when you do not answer a practice question correctly. In other words, to ensure that you have learned and will retain the content, successive relearning is a better option.

> *Rereading your textbook and notes can improve your retention, and rereading likely will have the largest impact when you space it across time. But retrieval practice over spaced intervals is still a more effective approach than rereading.*

On the basis of all the available evidence, we recommend that you use rereading sparingly. Of course, when you do not understand something, you may have no other option but to go back and reread to try to figure it out. If continued rereading fails to help you, however, then you will need to resort to more engaging strategies—such as studying examples of the content or asking a fellow student or an instructor for assistance.

SUMMARIZING

Summarizing as a strategy is exactly what it sounds like: briefly rephrasing the main points of what you are reading. On occasion, students will ask if they should copy their notes—just rewrite them to firmly store that content in their memory. We suspect that copying is not a good use of time because people can too easily just transcribe content without deeply engaging with it. By contrast, summarizing involves transforming the content and putting its meaning in your own words while trying to omit less important details and redundancies. Thus, compared with copying, writing a summary will be more engaging, so it seems like summarization is an excellent strategy for learning difficult content.

Unfortunately, research on the impact of summarization is not so encouraging, for a variety of reasons (for a review, see Dunlosky et al., 2013). First, the outcomes are mixed: Compared with students who just read texts, students who summarize them sometimes perform better, sometimes perform the same, and sometimes perform worse. Second, summarization itself can take quite a bit of time, perhaps as much or more than strategies like retrieval practice, which have been shown to consistently improve students' learning. Third, when younger students are trained to write excellent summaries, doing so does improve their learning, but even this encouraging outcome means that many students may need training to produce quality summaries so that summarization is an effective learning strategy for them.

IMAGERY

Your mind excels at transforming the information that your senses offer you. An amazing feat the mind can accomplish involves the use of mental images. Many people can recall images of what they've seen before or even transform other information—most notably, words—into an internal image that represents them. If you can, take a moment to mentally travel through a place that you know well, such as your home, and walk through it, making note of what is there. Most of us can develop detailed mental images of familiar places, and it almost feels as if we were there! Now, try to come up with a mental image of the word "dog." Maybe you are visualizing your own pet or a dog you saw on television recently. Now, visualize the word "spoon." If you put those two images together—perhaps you see a dog eating with a fancy spoon—then you are taking advantage of interactive imagery.

In fact, imagery was the go-to strategy among the first professional orators more than 2,000 years ago. Without paper available, orators would memorize lengthy tales to share with others: a feat that seems nearly impossible until you find out that these orators used effective mental strategies like the ones described here. One strategy that they used was highly effective and takes advantage of mental images like the ones that we encouraged you to generate. Called the *method of loci*, this strategy involves storing what you want to remember at different locations (or loci) that occur in a larger mental space. When you want to recall the information, you simply mentally travel back to each location. Orators would first commit to memory a theater with many locations (or stalls) and then store to-be-remembered content at different stalls for later retrieval.

For a more personal example, you would first identify distinct locations of a place you know well, such as the front door to your house, the coat rack in the entry hallway, the bedroom door that you then walk by, and so forth. At each location, you mentally place a to-be-remembered item. For instance, if you wanted to remember a list of groceries, you would place each grocery item in a different location of your house: apples at the front door, celery on the coat rack, broccoli hanging from the bedroom doorway, etc. Using mental images to make each visualized item interact with the location (like with dog–spoon in the earlier example) will help even more. For example, interactive images could be visualizing a huge red apple blocking the front door or a coat rack made out of celery. When you get to the grocery store, you would simply walk around your mental house to recall all the items you want to purchase.

The method of loci can be effective, but it may not be very practical to use in many cases. After all, you need to begin studying with loci already well memorized (which could take some time and effort), and much of the content you need to learn is not easily placed at locations. However, mental imagery can be a useful specialty tool as you become more sophisticated at applying each strategy just when you need it the most.

Why do we consider mental imagery a specialty strategy, whereas retrieval practice was considered to be a more general, all-purpose strategy? The answer to this question is that you can practice retrieving *any* content you want to learn, and doing so promises to boost your retention of it. By contrast, mental imagery works best when the content you are trying to learn is concrete; that is, the content is something that has a natural visual analog. A dog is concrete, and so are the geometries of molecules. However, much of the content you need to learn is abstract and hence cannot be easily transformed into an image. Despite this, not all abstract concepts are incompatible with this technique. For instance, when you are trying to learn the steps involved in photosynthesis, you could begin by visualizing a carbon dioxide molecule entering a plant leaf while the plant absorbs water through its roots, and so forth. Most textbooks would provide this visualization in the form of a figure, so why not attempt to visualize that figure using a real plant, rain, and the sun out on a perfect spring day? Your image of the perfect sun, spring rain shower, and favorite plant could itself become a theater of memory for attaching all the various players (carbon dioxide, oxygen, hydrogen molecules) in a chain from the beginning of the process to the end. You can try out visual imagery for any content that affords it, especially when you are struggling to retain that content using the more general strategies described in earlier chapters.

> *Mental imagery works best when the content you are trying to learn is concrete. But much of the content you need to learn is abstract and hence cannot be easily transformed into an image.*

Finally, consider one very specific application of this specialty tool: the *keyword mnemonic*. The keyword mnemonic is largely aimed at helping you learn to associate a foreign word with its translation equivalent, although it can be applied to learning the definitions of words and other more complex materials. For now, we consider an example with a foreign word pair. In French, the word "house" is *maison*. If you are just beginning to learn French, the word *maison* likely has no meaning to you and is not easily imaginable. To use this mnemonic, you would begin by generating a concrete keyword for *maison*; in this case, you may choose the term "mason." Next, you would form images of a "mason" (perhaps with a trowel in her hand) and an image of a house (perhaps one you lived in as a child). Then, form an interactive image of the two, such as the mason working on the bricks of the house. The idea is that when you later are asked for the meaning of *maison*, you recall the image of the highly related keyword "mason" working on a "house."

Pitfalls can arise when using this technique. A few experiments (e.g., Wang et al., 1992) have compared students who used the keyword mnemonic with a separate group who did not use it and merely studied the pairs of words. On an immediate test, performance was typically better for students who used the keyword mnemonic than for those who did not. On a test that was delayed, however, the reverse was found to be true: Those who used the keyword mnemonic forgot more of what they had learned! One reason is illustrated in the example we gave earlier: After a delay, you may correctly retrieve the keyword "mason" and the image of a mason working on the bricks of a house, but you may forget what the image was specifically linked to—does *maison* mean "house," or does it mean "brick"? In addition, it may take quite a bit of time and creativity to even figure out a keyword to use. If you're someone who enjoys developing stories and images, then maybe this will be a fun way to study, but we suspect most students would prefer using their time in other ways. Finally, open up an introductory textbook for almost any new language you may learn and many (if not most) of the foreign language words will not easily translate to keywords. Therefore, we recommend using this technique sparingly, perhaps for material that easily affords the generation of a meaningful keyword and interactive images.

HUDDLE UP

Anyone who tells you that they have an approach to studying that will make learning easy—or that magic will happen when you use, or at least buy, their learning technology—is just trying to get to your money. Learning is difficult, and it can also be frustrating when you spend a great deal of time studying yet make little progress. To study like a champion, you'll need to prepare yourself for the challenges of studying and choose the best study strategies to meet those challenges. We truly hope the last several chapters have inspired you to try out some of these strategies for yourself. We can guarantee that learning will still be difficult at times, but at least you will be making real progress and will have a path to mastery that is paved with effective strategies and the guidance of others—instructors, tutors, and friends—whenever you continue to struggle.

Key Training Tips

- Study Champions understand that learning is difficult and that no strategy exists that magically produces learning without effort.
- Sticking Your Landing involves using specialty strategies such as highlighting and imagery at the right time and for the right materials.

Go for the Gold With an Advanced Reading

Worthen, J. B., & Hunt, R. R. (2010). *Mnemonology: Mnemonics for the 21st century.* Taylor & Francis.

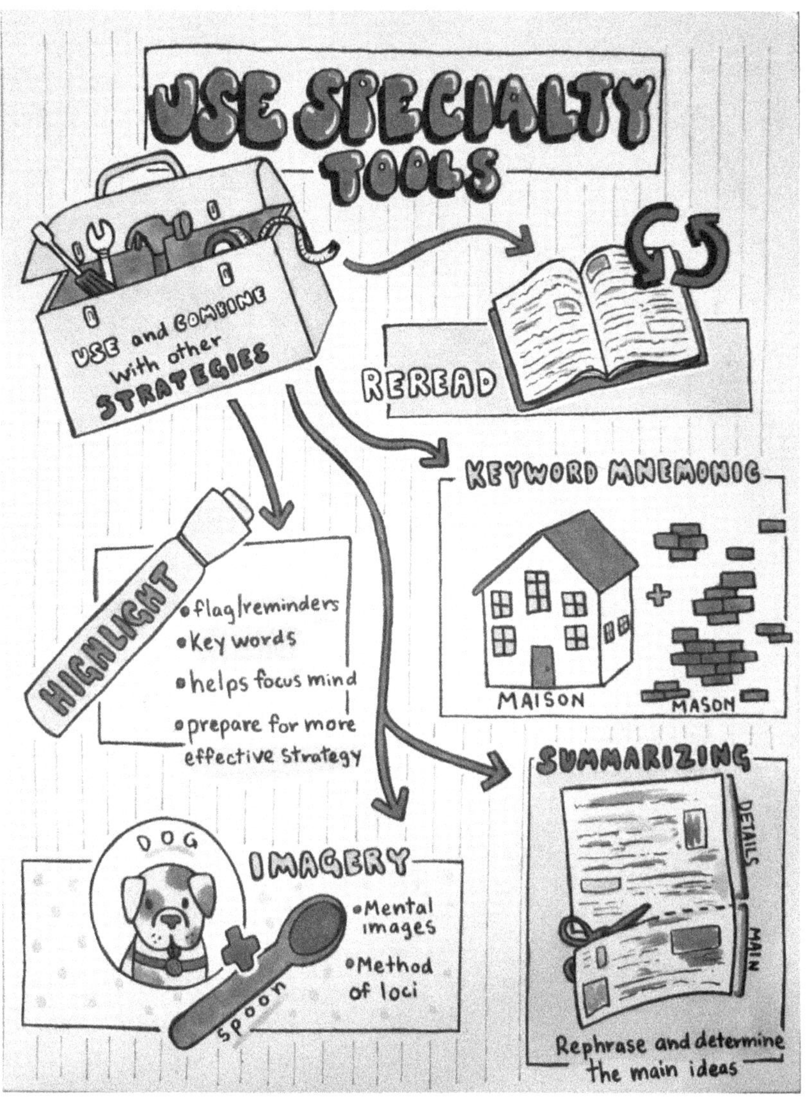

Drawing by Paige Herrboldt. Printed with permission.

CHAPTER 8

A QUICK LOOK AT SOMETHING NEW: MIXING AND MATCHING

In this chapter, you will learn

- that almost all study strategies have their place in your study toolbox,
- that mixing all-purpose and specialty strategies may be essential for learning some course content, and
- ideas on how to combine strategies to study like a champion.

Germaine has been diligently using successive relearning to prepare for an upcoming exam in an advanced course on cognitive psychology. They were making a great deal of progress on most concepts and retaining them well, but whenever they tried to recall the main assumptions of the levels-of-processing theory, their mind went blank. On the positive side, using successive relearning allowed Germaine to identify where they were struggling, but, on the negative side, they were struggling and frustrated. In this case, just restudying the assumptions after failing to retrieve them was not helping much. So, what can Germaine do to get over this learning obstacle? We have two immediate recommendations. First, although a failure may be frustrating, we recommend that you view it as a success of the learning process, which is difficult. The frustration is a sign that the learning objective has not yet been met. So, as you continue to use these strategies, try not to be frustrated, and instead regroup like a champion.

Our second recommendation is to regroup and combine successive relearning with another strategy. So, instead of merely rereading the feedback (i.e., the assumptions of the theory) after failing to recall the assumptions, consider using self-explanation (e.g., Why does levels-of-processing theory make these assumptions?), developing a mental image of some of the assumptions that afford it, or summarizing the assumptions in your own words.

The idea here is that even specialty strategies (and sometimes less effective ones), when applied appropriately, can be useful tools in your strategy toolbox, perhaps especially so when they are used with a more general strategy. In fact, at this point your toolbox should include an arsenal of strategies that you can trust and rely on, some of which you can apply more generally when learning almost any course content (e.g., retrieval practice) and others that are meant for more specific learning objectives (e.g., using worked examples). To study like a champion, you will often need to coordinate the use of multiple strategies to achieve your learning objectives. Given the number of strategies we've introduced, the number of possible combinations is rather daunting, so in the pages that follow we provide a few examples that can give you insight into how to develop the best combination for any new learning challenge.

Before we reveal some of our favorite combinations, we have an important caveat and a reminder. For the caveat, although a great deal of experimental research has focused on evaluating the benefits of the strategies described in this volume, this research has almost exclusively done so for one strategy in isolation. Little evidence is available about how well the strategies work in combination. So, the recommendations provided here are based on our informed intuitions that combining strategies will be useful for meeting your learning challenges. For the reminder, consider spaced practice again. Whereas most of the strategies we discuss prescribe *how* to go about studying, spaced practice prescribes *when* to go about studying—that is, spreading your review out over time. We point this out again because we encourage you to begin by developing a study schedule that involves spaced practice for each course, perhaps setting aside several sessions for each course per week. After you have developed your schedule, you need to decide which study strategy—or combination of strategies—best fits your learning needs for each study session.

While you are studying during a given session, some strategies can be particularly useful when they are used in conjunction with others; we list some of these strategy combinations in Exhibit 8.1. These examples illustrate only a few of the possible ways to combine strategies, so we encourage you to explore the strategy combinations that make the most sense for your current learning objectives. With that said, many of the strategy combinations are straightforward and self-explanatory, but we will highlight a few to make sure you understand how to use them with fidelity.

In regard to successive relearning, recall that it involves using retrieval practice with feedback until you correctly retrieve the desired content and then returning across multiple sessions to relearn the same content. As an aside, successive relearning itself is a combination of strategies: the appropriate use of retrieval practice and spaced practice. When you fail to correctly retrieve a sought-after answer, then you need to study (and attempt to learn) the correct answer. As the example of Germaine illustrates, you could simply reread the answer, but why not use a more engaging strategy while studying it? Consider using self-explanation to explain why the answer is correct (if appropriate), or perhaps develop a mental image of the answer (if it affords one). If you continue to struggle and just can't seem to get a particular answer to stick in memory well

EXHIBIT 8.1. Some Winning Strategy Combinations

Strategy combination	General approach
Highlighting plus any combination of effective strategies	Use highlighters to identify material to study
Successive relearning and self-explanation	Use self-explanation while restudying after a failed retrieval attempt
Successive relearning and imagery	Use imagery while restudying after a failed retrieval attempt
Interleaving and problem solving	Interleave different types of problems while problem solving
Worked examples and retrieval practice	Practice retrieving the steps of problems that you consistently forget
Worked examples and self-explanation	Explain why each step of a worked example is relevant to solving a problem
Rereading and self-explanation	When rereading, explain the most important content to yourself
Summarize plus successive relearning	After summarizing lengthy content, study it using another strategy
Summarize plus self-explanation	After summarizing lengthy content, study it using another strategy
Retrieval practice and help seeking	If you continue to struggle, seek help
Problem solving and help seeking	If you continue to struggle, seek help

enough to retrieve it, then you may not understand the answer well enough, perhaps because you lack the background knowledge or because a misconception is holding you back. But that's okay—successive relearning is a great strategy because it will allow you to monitor your progress with the most challenging material, and if you just can't seem to get it right, then it is probably a great time to seek help. For advice on doing so, please check out Chapter 9.

When you need to learn how to solve problems, using an interleaved schedule to practice problems while you study worked examples is a super combination. For the latter, when you are trying to solve problems but get stuck, it's a great time to study a worked example of the same kind of problem. For the former, interleaving is a schedule of practice that is particularly useful when combined with problem solving. Of course, it is important to make sure that you do not know in advance what specific kind of problem you are about to solve so that you can practice identifying each problem before you try to solve it.

When you are studying worked examples and subsequently trying to solve the problems on your own, you may realize that you consistently forget or fail to apply a step (or multiple steps) of a problem correctly. If you do, consider using a strategy that will help you remember that step in particular. For instance, before studying the next worked example, attempt to retrieve all the steps from memory and then evaluate whether you remembered them all. Another possibility is that you are struggling because you do not fully understand why each of the steps of a problem is necessary for obtaining a solution. To determine whether this is the case, why not attempt to explain the purpose of each step of a solution? If you cannot explain why a particular step is needed, then it may be time to return to your textbook or notes for the answers or to seek some advice from a fellow student or your instructor.

If you decide to summarize a lengthy section of a textbook to extract only the most important content, remember that doing so will probably not be sufficient to fully learn that content. So, after summarizing, consider using some of the more effective strategies to really learn the content. After summarizing, can you explain the summary to yourself? If not, perhaps your summary is not complete, or maybe you need to refer to other materials (another textbook or your notes) to help you understand the content well enough to explain it. You could also use successive relearning by figuring out which aspects of the content should serve as retrieval cues and what content you want to be able to retrieve from memory, and then use the summary like you would use successive relearning with flash cards. These are just a few examples of how to combine these strategies, and you may find that some work better for you.

Our recommendation is that you use the strategies flexibly and keep at it until you meet your learning objectives. In other words, you should be trying to evaluate or monitor your progress toward your ultimate goal, which brings us to our final point: After multiple study sessions, you will need to decide whether you have met your learning objectives, and a great way to do this is with a practice test. If the goal involves solving a certain type of problem, then practice solving those problems until you can do so correctly. If the exam involves describing the Krebs cycle, then attempt to describe it by writing it down from memory. If you cannot do so during your study session, then you haven't yet met your learning objective—and even if you can successfully recall it during a given study session, you will likely forget aspects of it afterward, so try recalling it again during a different study session. The main idea is to try to figure out how you are expected to use the material you are studying on the exam—whether it be answering multiple-choice questions, completing essays, performing some procedure, or solving problems—and to continue practicing what you are expected to do until you have achieved mastery. When you are finally confronted with your high-stakes exam, you will know that you are ready for it, because you've been learning the content in a way that will allow you to excel.

Now that we have presented some tips about how to combine study strategies to meet your learning objectives, we also need to emphasize that being a successful student involves more than just studying. Other habits—such as how much you sleep and whether you exercise—can contribute to your performance, happiness, and overall well-being. In addition, you need to remember that you're not alone on your journey to succeed in school. When needed, you should seek out the advice and assistance of fellow students, mentors, tutors, and instructors. Accordingly, we use our final chapter to talk about other excellent habits for Study Champions and offer some advice on how to seek help from others.

HUDDLE UP

How should you study like a champion? Begin by selecting the most general study technique to prepare for a course: Develop a plan and manage your time to schedule weekly study sessions; then, choose from the all-purpose strategies to use during each study session, perhaps planning to highlight the most critical material you need to learn; read it all using self-explanation; and then apply successive relearning for the content you need to retain for the exams. Next, if you continue to struggle with some material, search your study toolbox for a specialty strategy appropriate for the current challenge. Use imagery if you are having difficulties retaining concrete information, explain why each step to solve a difficult problem is necessary for its solution, and even seek help from friends in the class or from your instructor. Although studying like a champion may require practice before it is mastered, this approach is itself rather straightforward: Figure out what your learning objectives are for a class, and then spend some time soon after the first day of class to plan how to meet those objectives and to choose the best strategies to meet them effectively.

Key Training Tips

- Study Champions combine general learning strategies with specialty strategies.
- Sticking Your Landing involves considering what you are trying to master and choosing the right combination of strategies.

Go for the Gold With an Advanced Reading

Miyatsu, T., Nguyen, K., & McDaniel, M. A. (2018). Five popular study strategies: Their pitfalls and optimal implementations. *Perspectives on Psychological Science*, *13*(3), 390–407. https://doi.org/10.1177/1745691617710510

Drawing by Paige Herrboldt. Printed with permission.

III

BEYOND THE CLASSROOM

CHAPTER 9

THE A(FFECT), B(EHAVIORS), AND C(OGNITIONS) OF CHAMPIONS

I sometimes drink so much I pass out and do not remember what happened next.

—"Matthew," a former student of ours

In this chapter, you will learn

- why healthy behaviors are essential to getting good grades,
- some of the best ways to cope with college life and stress, and
- why good eating and getting physical (activity) can be game changers.

Matthew's quote opens this chapter, and he was not boasting—he was embarrassed, but blunt, as he shared this information with the rest of his health psychology class. When pushed, he shared that he goes out drinking with his friends four to five nights per week. At each session, they would start at one friend's apartment and do a round of drinks. They would then go to another friend's place and have some more drinks and then go to a local establishment that served cheap alcohol. Matthew acknowledged this may be the reason many of his assignments are late, that he had forgotten to turn in a paper, and that he had failed a midterm. Matthew also smoked when he drank. Given his social life, he did not go to bed until 3:00 a.m. on most nights. Drinking is only the tip of the iceberg of Matthew's problems. Do you know any "Matthew"s?

Studying like a champion takes more than practicing and mastering the different techniques we have laid out in the preceding chapters. Learning well, getting high grades in class, and retaining that knowledge over a long period of time will also involve taking good care of your mental and physical health. You will sometimes hear this in class or in an orientation to college seminar. Most of the time, faculty focus on what to study and urge you to keep up with readings and assignments (two critical elements, of course), at the expense of taking a holistic view. To be successful at what we do, and to be happier, we need to focus on the whole person. The *whole person* includes our feelings (or affect), our actions (or behaviors), and our thoughts (or cognitions). These are the fundamental ABCs of being a Study Champion, and in this chapter, we focus on how to keep those optimal.

In this chapter, we provide an overview of four major physical health behaviors—eating, drinking, physical activity, and sleep—and a major psychological health behavior called *mindfulness*. Together, these five behaviors will help you truly study like a champion.

Start Now: Assess Yourself

The following set of questions was designed to measure your health behaviors. For each item, indicate the extent to which you perform the behavior, with 1 = *not at all* and 5 = *all the time*. After you read all the questions and list a value, reflect on your answers.

1. _____ I exercise to stay healthy.
2. _____ I eat a balanced diet.
3. _____ I take vitamins.
4. _____ I see a dentist for regular checkups.
5. _____ I watch my weight.
6. _____ I limit my intake of foods like coffee, sugar, and fats.
7. _____ I gather information on things that affect my health.
8. _____ I watch for possible signs of major health problems.

9. ______ I take health supplements.
10. ______ I see a doctor for regular checkups.
11. ______ I use dental floss regularly.
12. ______ I discuss health with friends, neighbors, and relatives.
13. ______ I don't smoke.
14. ______ I brush my teeth regularly.
15. ______ I get shots to prevent illness.
16. ______ I get enough sleep.

Now calculate the total of your scores. The closer you are to 80, the healthier you are.

Note. From "The Health Behavior Checklist: Factor Structure in Community Samples and Validity of a Revised Good Health Practices Scale," by S. E. Hampson, G. W. Edmonds, and L. R. Goldberg, 2019, *Journal of Health Psychology*, *24*(8), p. 1111 (https://doi.org/10.1177/1359105316687629). Copyright by 2019 by Sage. Reprinted with permission.

KEY CONSIDERATIONS IN BEING HEALTHY

There are many ways health is defined, especially across cultures, but here is a comprehensive and short definition: *Health* is a state of complete physical, mental, and social well-being (Gurung, 2019). The description includes a physical component, which is what comes to mind for most people when they think about being healthy. To be physically healthy, you need to ensure you are doing what science has shown is effective at making and keeping you healthy. Even though there seems to be a new study and related health behavior suggestion every week, there are some prescriptions that have been consistently supported by science. These include avoiding hazardous behaviors (e.g., smoking, texting while driving), getting enough sleep, eating well, limiting alcohol, and getting enough physical activity. This broad definition of health also includes a mental component, which is particularly important to studying like a champion and includes how you cope with stress and practice mindfulness.

It is important to see health as a continuum with optimal health at one end and poor health at the other. This means that at any given point in time you are at a specific place on that continuum, and any changes in your behavior can move you toward one of the two ends. If you start being more physically active, you move toward the healthy end. If you begin smoking or eating poorly, you move to the unhealthy end.

Let's walk you through some key prescriptions that will help you study like a champion. You may look at some of the subheadings and think you have that behavior down. Do not skip the section—elements of each one may surprise you.

GET ENOUGH SLEEP

We start with sleep because this is perhaps the most commonly abused health behavior in college. Most college students we talk to do not seem to get enough sleep. The national data also seem to support this observation. The Centers for Diseases Control and Prevention (2017) suggests adults ages 18 to 60 should get at least 7 hours of sleep a night, but they also estimate that more than 35% of adults are not managing to do so.

Sleep serves many important functions, and getting enough is very important. In general, sleep is the time our body uses to rebuild. Examinations of sleep activity show this is the time for protein growth, cell rebuilding, and even the cleansing of toxins. In regard to studying, evidence suggests that when you sleep you consolidate your memories from the day before. This has some pretty key implications. Sleeping right after studying actually helps you remember what you studied better for an exam than if you woke up early to study just before an exam. Of course, not cramming the night before and spacing out your studying are even better (see Chapter 5).

How you feel in the morning is related to both how much you sleep and whether your sleep cycle is consistent. An optimal pattern is that you go to bed and wake up at the same time every day of the week—even if that means you are going to bed at 1:00 a.m. and waking up at 9:00 a.m. daily. You are getting 8 hours of sleep, and you are doing it consistently (although class and work schedules may not allow this). The consistency is important because we all have a *circadian*, or daily body, rhythm. Our body secretes hormones and other chemicals on the basis of our sleep–wake schedules. Our temperature changes in accordance with those same schedules. Just before we wake up, there is a spike in chemical release that prepares us for action. If we keep changing the time when we wake up, this spike does not match our activities. For optimal health and alertness, you need to get enough sleep, and you need to maintain a consistent sleep cycle. Staying out late to party two to three nights a week and sleeping in, then going to bed relatively earlier and waking up for class early on only some days, disrupts your circadian rhythm.

> *For optimal health and alertness, you need to get enough sleep, and you need to maintain a consistent sleep cycle.*

Here are a few more critical points. How much sleep is enough varies across people. Eight hours a night is a safe average. Some people may need more than that, and a few may need less. Even more important, the quality of sleep is significant too. Not only is higher sleep quality related to better health and lower levels of depression, but also, the better the quality of your sleep, the less sleepy you feel the next day (Pilcher & Morris, 2020). Sleep and waking are heavily reliant on the amount of light around. If you want to sleep well, sleep in the dark. If you do not have good curtains, consider an eye mask. Also, make sure there are few sounds around, and, even if you are someone who uses your phone as your alarm clock, turn your phone off when you sleep: Get a $10 clock instead. If your phone is next to you, or under your pillow, a large part of your awareness will be monitoring the phone. You will be attuned to notifications. Many students wake up in the night and sleep-text (respond to texts and not even remember they did it in the morning). This sleep-texting or waking to a notification can wreak havoc on sleep quality. Do what you can to decouple yourself from your phone when you sleep. You will sleep more restfully, which will pay off in the form of fewer sleepy days and more focus and attention.

WATCH YOUR STRESS LEVELS

Stress is a different thing to different people. One easy way to think about stress is as something that upsets your body's balance, or *homeostasis*. Our body has a preferred level of functioning with settings for temperature, blood sugar level, body temperature, breathing, and blood pressure. There is a familiar physical analogy. Most houses in North America have a thermostat, designed to maintain its optimal level in all areas of functioning. We set our thermostats, and if the temperature drops below the set level, the house is heated. If the temperature rises, the house is cooled, and a constant temperature is maintained. Our bodies have a brain structure called the *hypothalamus* that serves the same function. The hypothalamus ensures that our bodies maintain a set level. Anything that stresses our systems tends to tip this fine balance.

When you get stressed, various body systems activate to help you deal with the stressor. Your heart rate goes up, circulation increases, and your breathing increases. Some bodily systems also get turned down or off. Stress can influence digestion and reproduction.

You note this by changes in your eating behaviors and, for women, fluctuations in the menstrual system. There may be changes in sexual desire as well (e.g., a lack of interest). These changes reflect the complex interplay of physical and mental factors when you get stressed, which is why coping well is important.

All of us face demands that can produce a lot of stress. For the average college student, there are course readings and assignments, classes to attend, and exams to study for. Each class can be challenging, and when you factor in taking multiple classes, the stress can get worse. In addition, many students also have to work. At work, many encounter more deadlines, as well as training, and, in some cases, the pressure to sell quotas or hit market targets.

In addition to the academic and work spheres, there is the personal sphere. Friends and family can be a great source of happiness and pleasure, but you may also have many people who lean on you and count on you for support and help, whether emotional, physical, or financial. Varying expectations, deadlines, and situations can singularly and collectively all serve as potential stressors.

Stress means different things to different people, and the same can be said of coping. Health psychologists define *coping* as what we do to reduce or prevent the harm, threats, or loss that accompany stressors and reduce associated distress (Carver & Connor-Smith, 2010). There are many specific ways people cope with stress. Some turn to religion and pray. Some distract themselves. Some may indulge in drugs or alcohol. Others may face the stressors head on. Some of these styles are more effective than others, but the reality is that the best coping strategy depends on the type of stressor, whether it is controllable, and whether it is long term or short term. Coping researchers made all this variety slightly easier to understand when they found that human coping can first be divided into two large groups: (a) *approach*, or *problem-focused* coping and (b) *avoidant*, or *emotion-focused* coping.

You can decide to tackle a stressful event head-on and resolve it; this is approach coping. Alternatively, you can work to avoid it; this is avoidant coping. For example, if you dislike your job and your coworkers, going to work can be stressful. You could speak to your supervisor and improve your working conditions. This would be an approach style. Of course, you could just call in sick often and stay away from your job; now you would be using avoidant coping. You can avoid stress either through behavior (e.g., not going in to work) or mental efforts (e.g., by distracting yourself with Netflix bingeing). Researchers have examined each type of coping as distinct from one another, but in practice both styles are interwoven with each other, with one often complementing the other.

> *We often get stressed when we have too much to do. Planning well helps cut down on this.*

The good news is that many of the chapters in this book provide advice on how to cope with the demands of being a student. Planning (and time management), discussed in Chapter 2, is a great way to cope that helps prevent deadlines from creeping up and becoming major stressors. We often get stressed when we have too much to do. Planning well helps cut down on this. Imagine being finished with projects before deadlines and knowing the course material a couple days before an exam. That will reduce stress for sure.

GET SOCIAL SUPPORT

A line from one of our favorite Beatles songs nicely captures years of health psychology research: "I get by with a little help from my friends." Indeed, one of our most important resources is the people around us who care about us. Our success at coping with stress is heavily dependent on the quality and quantity of support we actually get or even believe we can get. Yes, even believing there are many people who can support us can keep us healthier and stress free. *Social support* is most commonly defined as the feeling of being loved and cared for; it can take the form of emotional, informational, or instrumental assistance from others. Social support may be one of the best elements to cultivate in college life, especially when you feel stressed and you reach out to friends and family members. Take the time to text, email, call, or video chat with those you care about no matter how close or far they are. Cultivating your networks and keeping in touch with friends is a big part of coping with stress in college.

Social support also helps us cope with mental health issues and feeling burned out. Mental health issues on campus have risen to new highs over the past few years (Hoyt et al., 2021). In fact, one study showed that mental health diagnoses rose from 22% in 2007 to more than 35% just 10 years later (Lipson et al., 2019). Too many students who need help with mental health do not seek it, and instructors can make a big difference. As we discussed in Chapter 3, students often are resistant to even reach out to their instructors for course-related problems. If you do not understand something in the textbook, or you want more clarification on what you took notes on, you may appreciate having the instructor's slides or lecture notes. You should reach out. Many students are reluctant to do this, but we urge you to try it. Your faculty want you to succeed, and they can be a critical source of support. Reaching out can be done many ways. Use their office hours. If you do not want to go in person, they may be open to a chat on Zoom. Email them. Although few faculty text or use social media (e.g., Instagram) to communicate with students, all of them use email, which is an easy way to get in touch. You can get a good sense of how best to communicate with your professor from their syllabus (Gurung & Galardi, 2021). A syllabus may also have different options for you to get help for issues not directly related to class, such as if you are feeling anxious or depressed.

Whether it is stress, anxiety, or feeling low that is a problem, practicing mindfulness is also a great way to relax, and it can help you learn, two benefits that interact with each other.

PRACTICE MINDFULNESS

We live in a chaotic world that is made more so by our easy access to information. You can be sitting in the most idyllic, beautiful, restful setting, but if you have your phone with you and it's on, you likely will be awash in messages and notifications. Text notifications compete for your attention. You may want to check how many likes you got on Instagram or your other favorite social media platform. There may be gossip, rumors about your favorite personalities or sports teams on Twitter, or the latest post from some political pundit. It is easy to be distracted. Even if you are not out on a mountain or lakeside, but in your room at your computer, you may still have multiple browser windows open. A class Learning Management System may be competing with YouTube videos or a shopping channel. A key skill is developing focus.

We talked about the importance of attention and the perils of divided attention way back in Chapter 1. Now we address how to develop even more explicit skills for you, so you can direct your attention and sustain it. This ability to home in on one aspect of life at a time is a crucial cognitive capacity related to academic achievement. The father of psychology in the United States, William James (1890), famously said that "the faculty of voluntarily bringing back a wandering attention, over and over again, is the very root of judgment, character, and will. . . . An education which should improve this faculty would be the education par excellence" (p. 424). Mindfulness is the answer.

There are diverse ways to describe mindfulness. At its most essential level, to practice mindfulness you need to pay close attention to your conscious experiences from moment to moment and then monitor that attention to keep focused on the present (Gallant, 2016). Like a wild monkey in the tropical rainforests of Asia, our minds easily jump from thought to thought, wandering, distracted by this and that. When you practice mindfulness you aim to recognize both internal and external distractors, whether thoughts or sounds, and pull your attention back to the present without judgment. Jon Kabat-Zinn, the most well-known proponent of mindfulness as a stress reliever, describes mindfulness as the awareness that arises from paying attention on purpose, in the present moment, and without judgment (Kabat-Zinn, 2003).

Once relegated to the New Age sections of bookstores and thought to be the realm of sages and yogis, mindfulness has been in the American mainstream for many years now. In fact, mindfulness-based programs have been developed by countries across the world (Waters et al., 2015). Mindfulness training, in college settings in particular, reduces stress and anxiety; improves psychological well-being, sleep quality, and mood; and improves a number of different cognitive abilities, such as working memory and cognitive flexibility (Calma-Birling & Gurung, 2017).

If you need convincing, take note of some of the studies that have demonstrated the positive effects of mindfulness. In one study, students participated in 10 minutes of mindfulness practice twice a week, and 15 weeks later they showed higher levels of self-compassion, had lower levels of perceived stress and anxiety, and ruminated less (Yamada & Victor, 2012). In another study, students who participated in a 6-minute mindfulness training scored better on the postlecture quiz compared with students who did not practice mindfulness (Ramsburg & Youmans, 2014).

So, why should you practice mindfulness? Mindfulness seems to relate to immediate increases in memory capacity, which may be related to its effects on cutting down on distraction and mind wandering. Practicing mindfulness sharpens your ability to pay attention, in particular, by helping you notice when your mind wanders (Mrazek et al., 2013). By helping you repeatedly bring your attention back to what you are trying to focus on, mindfulness helps you develop sustained attention (Morrison et al., 2014). You learn how to not let thoughts, emotions, or body sensations hijack your awareness of the present moment. This self-regulation of attention (see Chapter 2) is, in essence, what practicing mindfulness urges. It activates specific cognitive processes, such as sustained attention (i.e., the ability to focus attention on a certain stimulus for an extended period of time without becoming distracted), cognitive flexibility (i.e., the ability to shift the focus of attention in response to contextual demands), and cognitive inhibition (i.e., the ability to suppress automatic responses that interfere with current demands; Burley et al., 2022).

When you are studying, attention regulation is supremely important. When you are in class and perhaps become distracted during a lecture (e.g., an incoming text message, mind wandering), you need to be able to bring your attention back to class. Research has documented that your attention decreases as time passes in a lecture setting. The longer the lecture, the more likely you are to pay less attention. Mindfulness helps you pay attention longer, and the more you practice the better your attention levels will be.

Try this easy way to get things done; it is referred to as the *Pomodoro method*, so named after a tomato-shaped kitchen timer. You set the timer of your choice (it does not have to be a tomato) for 20 minutes. Then you get working, with a commitment to keep working until the timer goes off. In the event you are not focused on the task when it rings (e.g., you are watching TikTok), reorient yourself to the task. Then, reset the timer. If you are on task, set the timer for 30 minutes and start again until you are always on task when the timer goes off. This is a particularly good technique when you are working on a task you don't want to do.

You can try some mindfulness right now. Jacob Lindsley and Kate Gallagher, two mindfulness experts at Oregon State University, gave us permission to share three different sets of instructions. These practices are designed especially for college students. Try them.

Awareness of Breathing

- Decide how long you'd like to practice, and set a timer.
- Place your body in a comfortable position, with your back upright.
- Take a few deep breaths to release any unnecessary hardness or tension in the body, then let your breath fall into a natural rhythm.
- Acknowledge any sounds in the room, bodily sensations, and thoughts that are moving in and out of your awareness. They will continue to come and go in the background, or periphery.
- For a time, notice that you're breathing; notice the sensations of breath.
- Rest your attention on the sensations of breathing at *one* location in the body: the belly, the chest, or the nostrils. Notice the sensations of the flow of breath there: in and out.
- Attune to, and attend to, the breath.
- When your attention is captured by a narrative, planning, or worry, rejoice that you've noticed, and return your attention to the sensations of breath at the location of your choice.
- Continue until the timer sounds.

Body Scan

- Decide how long you'd like to practice, and set a timer.
- Place your body in a comfortable position, with your back upright.

- Take a few deep breaths to release any unnecessary hardness or tension in the body, then let your breath fall into a natural rhythm.
- Acknowledge any sounds in the room, bodily sensations, and thoughts that are moving in and out of your awareness. They will continue to come and go in the background or periphery.
- Begin to "scan" your body by focusing your attention on specific places, starting at the lowest part of your body and working your way to the top. Spend time noticing the sensations of the following:
  - your left foot and your right foot
  - your left lower leg and your right lower leg
  - your left upper leg and your right upper leg
  - your pelvis and seat
  - your lower back
  - your belly
  - your chest
  - your upper back
  - your left shoulder, upper arm, elbow, lower arm, wrist, hand, and fingers
  - your right shoulder, upper arm, elbow, lower arm, wrist, hand, and fingers
  - your neck
  - your head
  - your face
- When your attention is captured by a narrative, planning, or worry, rejoice that you've noticed, and return your attention to the body part you were previously working with. For the rest of the duration, let your attention roam throughout your body, noticing any physical sensations as they arise and abate. Continue until the timer sounds.

Open Awareness

- Decide how long you'd like to practice, and set a timer.
- Place your body in a comfortable position, with your back upright.
- Take a few deep breaths to release any unnecessary hardness or tension in the body, then let your breath fall into a natural rhythm.
- Let your awareness open wide to the sensory experience of being alive in the present moment.
- Take in the sounds in the room.
- Notice thoughts coming and going.
- Feel the sensations throughout your body.
- Be aware of the rhythm of your breath.
- Sounds, thoughts, body, breath. Take them all in. Notice how each arises and abates.
- When your attention narrows and is captured by a narrative, planning, or worry, rejoice that you've noticed, relax on the out breath, and open your awareness to the sounds in the room.
- Sounds, thoughts, body, breath: Take them all in. Notice how each comes and goes.
- Continue until the timer sounds.

Can even a brief intervention help? Destany Calma-Birling, a senior psychology major, and Regan answered this question (Calma-Birling & Gurung, 2017). They examined whether 5 minutes of mindfulness practice can increase learning. Destany taught one group of participants how to practice focused-attention meditation and compared their quiz scores. This group began class by listening to Destany deliver a 12-minute PowerPoint presentation on mindfulness relative to education. After her presentation, students watched the 6-minute video on focused-attention meditation described earlier and were invited to engage in a 5-minute mindfulness exercise. A comparison group began class by watching an 18-minute video on racial discrimination in everyday life. After the video, the instructor proceeded as normal with the lecture. The following week, students in both classes took a quiz on the lecture content of that day. The students who engaged in 5 minutes mindfulness practice performed significantly better on the quizzes compared with students in the control group (see Figure 9.1).

Are you curious about what the mindfulness practice involved? Students were first told to voluntarily direct and sustain their attention on a specific component (e.g., their breath). They were told

FIGURE 9.1. Means, Standard Deviations, and Effect Size for Major Dependent Measures

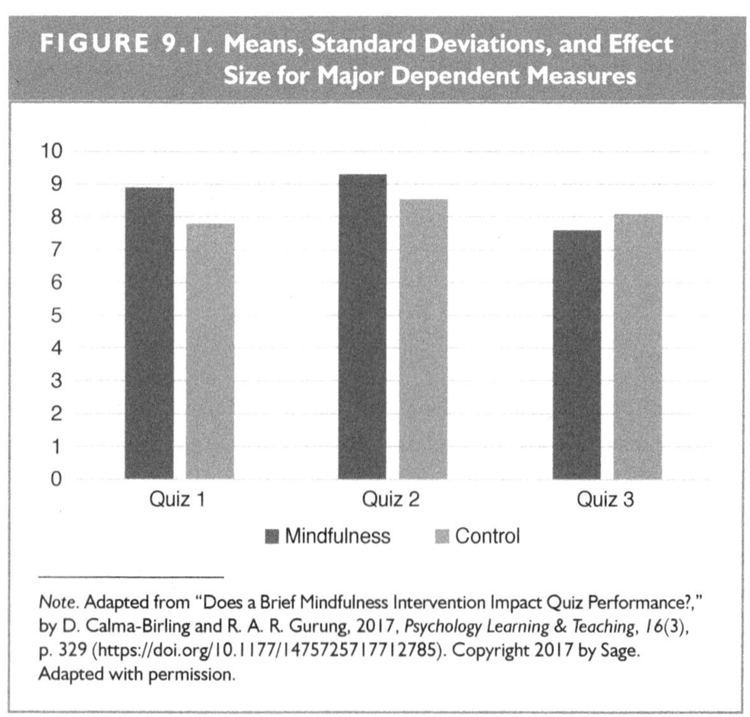

Note. Adapted from "Does a Brief Mindfulness Intervention Impact Quiz Performance?," by D. Calma-Birling and R. A. R. Gurung, 2017, *Psychology Learning & Teaching, 16*(3), p. 329 (https://doi.org/10.1177/1475725717712785). Copyright 2017 by Sage. Adapted with permission.

to try to recognize whether and when they got distracted. When they caught their mind wandering, they were told to reorient attention away from distractors and shift attention back to their breath. Finally, they were taught to see the distractor as "just a thought" and go easy on themselves, saying, "It is okay to be distracted" (Lutz et al., 2008). You can try the focused-attention meditation they used, a 6-minute video-clip by Jeffrey M. Schwartz (see https://www.youtube.com/watch?v=oH1H3eC_KFE).

EAT SMART

You may think that eating some foods, such as a pint of your favorite ice cream or a double serving of chicken wings, makes you feel better. This does not seem to be the case. Researchers examined what makes us feel better and experimentally compared different types of food options (Troisi & Gabriel, 2011). First, participants completed an online survey and listed foodstuffs they ate that made them feel good. The most commonly mentioned comfort foods were chocolate (26%), ice cream (18%), and cookies (11%). At least a week after they completed the surveys, participants came into the research laboratory and watched films that made them feel low. In a number of different studies, the participants then got to eat their comfort food, no food, or some other food item. Eating the comfort food did make participants feel better, but so did eating the noncomfort food, or no food. In essence, mood got better as the time from watching the film increased regardless of whether food (comfort or not) was eaten.

Are you eating a balanced diet? What *is* a balanced diet? You know all about the three main macronutrients (proteins, carbohydrates, and fats), but how much you should eat of each is often debated. Some research has suggested that a high-protein diet with few to no carbohydrates is best. Other research suggests that, no matter what, just eating less (smaller serving sizes of whatever you pick) is best. We know the realities of college life. Students often eat food with a lot of carbohydrates (pizza and pasta) and will be tempted to eat late in the night and at different hours of the day. Unfortunately, eating too many carbs and eating late in the night can lead to weight gain, which is also associated with frequent consumption of fast foods, sugar-sweetened drinks, food prepared outside the home, alcohol, and large portion sizes (Halliday et al., 2019). Weight gain can also have health consequences over the long term.

Like any competition, what you eat and how you fuel your body can influence your performance. Most important to the theme of this book is the fact that eating well is important to learning. In particular, different types of foods provide energy in different ways. If you eat a heavy-protein breakfast, your energy levels will actually stay higher longer. A doughnut or a bagel may be quick and easy, the latter even seeming healthy, but the carbs in these two items break down quickly: You get a shot of energy quick, but you also get hungry sooner. The current state of research supports Pollan's (2007) suggestion to eat food that is natural and minimally processed, mostly green, and to not each too much. As far as diets go, the only contender seems to be the Mediterranean diet, which includes a lot of vegetables and nuts. If you enjoy Greek food (e.g., tabbouleh, hummus), you have already had a taste for this type of food. This diet includes limiting meat and eating more fish, whole grains, and vegetables.

GET PHYSICAL ACTIVITY

Most people know that exercise is good for their physical health. It is also good for mental health and learning. Physical activity can reduce symptoms of depression and anxiety and increase self-esteem. It confers many physical and psychological benefits, including lowered blood pressure, weight loss, stress reduction, and increased self-confidence. Being inactive (e.g., sitting for long periods of time) is independently associated with a wide array of health risks, such as weight gain, problems with attention, loss of focus, irritability, and lethargy (Lieberman, 2021).

The U.S. Department of Health and Human Services (2018) suggests that each of us should take part in at least moderate-intensity physical activity on most days of the week. Adults (ages 18 to 65) should engage in 150 minutes of moderate-intensity, or 75 minutes of high-intensity, activity per week. A key aspect to note is that this activity can be a combination of 10-minute episodes spread through the week. The guidelines also suggest doing muscle strengthening activities for all muscle groups at least twice a week. When people think about the recommendations for physical activity, they often picture going to a gym, running, biking, or lifting weights, but you can expend energy and be physically active in many other ways. Even walking and standing burn energy. It is easy to spend long periods of time at a desk working on a computer, so consider spending some of that time standing as well. Make sure you take breaks often and go for a walk around the block. Moving around the house or campus, playing sports, dancing, or walking as a leisure activity all burn energy. When you create your plan for the week (see Chapter 2), add a workout.

Being fit involves many aspects of health. If you want to be healthier (especially given that it helps you study and learn better), make sure you practice the different areas of fitness. Just running, or just lifting weights, or just swimming focuses on only one aspect of fitness. There are many areas in which you can aim to improve your fitness level. *Cardiovascular endurance*, often referred to as *aerobic fitness*, refers to the body's capacity to take in, transport, and utilize oxygen. A common measure of aerobic fitness is the volume of oxygen (VO_2) a person uses while performing different tasks. Running and swimming can build this form of endurance. There are many other components of fitness as well. Muscular strength, muscular endurance, muscular power, speed, flexibility, agility, balance, good reaction times, and a low percentage of body fat are other components used to assess fitness. When you plan on incorporating physical activity into your week, try your best to get many of these activities in there.

LIMIT DRINKING

Matthew, who is quoted at the onset of this chapter, clearly has a habit of drinking too much. Whether drinking alcohol is a good thing or a bad thing has probably stimulated more spirited conversations than any other health behavior topic. Smoking is dangerous, there is no question, but is drinking? The government recommendation is that men can consume two drinks per day, and women can consume one drink per day, without significant negative health effects (U.S. Department of Agriculture & U.S. Department of Health and Human Services, 2020). You have also probably had friends justify their drinking by citing research concluding that a drink per day is actually *better* than no drinks at all. Is this true?

At most colleges, alcohol abuse is evident. Nearly half of college students are binge drinkers, that is, men who have consumed five or more drinks in a row and women who have consumed four or more drinks in a row at least once during the previous 2 weeks (Erblich, 2019). The proportion of current drinkers who binge is highest in the 18- to 20-year-old group (51%). The bad news is that alcohol consumption is responsible for more than 100,000 deaths each year, the third-leading cause of death after smoking and insufficient physical activity/and poor diet.

Alcohol is not good for learning. It is clear now that drinking, especially if you are underage, could hurt how you learn, remember, and process information. A report that compiled several studies on brain damage and alcohol concluded that underage drinkers face a greater risk of damage to the prefrontal regions of their brains. Double the amount of alcohol is required to do the same damage to someone older than 21. The development of the frontal lobes continues until age 16, after which the brain maintains a high rate of energy expenditure that does not decrease until age 20 (Robles et al., 2019). Underage drinking does retard brain cell growth, and neurons in the brains of underage drinkers actually fire differently from neurons in the brains of nondrinkers during memory and learning tasks (Zeigler et al., 2005).

While previous reports have shown evidence of benefits to small or moderate amounts of alcohol consumption, new research shows even moderate drinking can be associated with heart problems and failure (European Society of Cardiology, 2022). Yet, higher levels of high-density lipoprotein cholesterol help keep the arteries free of blockage, but nondrinkers older than 21 should not start drinking if they have not so far. There is simply not enough clinical and epidemiological evidence for science to recommend the consumption of alcohol to those who abstain.

HUDDLE UP

Learning is a challenging business. We hope you have the sense that getting good grades in class, and learning for life in general, requires a lot more than just "working hard." Of course, effort is important. You will need to be motivated or get motivated. You now know about effective ways to excel in your classes, including planning, managing your time, and using the most effective study schedules and strategies. To become a Study Champion, of course, you'll need to begin embracing this approach to studying. However, if necessary, you should also begin treating yourself better, such as by getting a consistent good night's sleep and some physical activity every day.

College is challenging; Life in general is as well. Practicing the different techniques we have described in this book will get you well on your way to being a Study Champion. To get all the metacognitive elements of that work in line and functioning, you also need to be healthy. You need to eat and drink well, sleep well, be physically active, and cope well with stress. Being healthy is useful in college and beyond. Does that sound like a tall order? Sure. Can you do it? We know you can. All the best.

Key Training Tips

- Study Champions take a holistic approach to health and try to get enough sleep, eat well, limit drinking, and get sufficient physical activity.
- Sticking Your Landing includes adding one of the best practices to help cope with stress and increase your performance: mindfulness. Find a practice that works well for you.

Go for the Gold With an Advanced Reading

Lieberman, D. E. (2021). *Exercised: Why something we never evolved to do is healthy and rewarding*. Pantheon.

Drawing by Paige Herrboldt. Printed with permission.

APPENDIX

CHAMPIONSHIP PRACTICE EXERCISES

Here are some key resources and exercises for you to hone your championship study skills.

TEST YOUR KNOWLEDGE

Look over this list of 12 study strategies. Some of these are better than others, as determined by years of research. Circle the best practices. (The answer is given at the very end of this appendix.)

1. Reading the material over and over
2. Spreading out your studying over many days
3. Staying up late the night before to pull an all-nighter
4. Using flash cards to test your knowledge
5. Cramming right before the test
6. Mixing up material from different classes rather than studying for just one class at a time
7. Rewriting your notes
8. Coming up with questions to test your understanding
9. Memorizing definitions of key terms
10. Applying the information to your own life
11. Making the material fit your personal learning style
12. Studying in a quiet place with no distractions

SEE HOW MULTITASKING IS COSTLY

Find a friend to help you out, and then time each other as you do the following:

1. As quickly as you can, count down from 10 to 0, then immediately say the alphabet out loud from A through K.
2. Now, alternate between the alphabet and counting down, 10–A, 9–B, and so on.
3. Divide your second task time by your first time.

Take a look at the ratio you got in Step 3. If your ratio is 1 or less, you are good at multitasking. If your ratio is greater than 1, it indicates how much slower you were at multitasking. For example, a 3.0 means you were 3 times slower multitasking than focusing on one task at a time.

Think about which task was easier and observe whether your experience matches your times.

- Consider how much more inefficient you are while multitasking than focusing on one topic and then another. Note that these are familiar, highly overlearned tasks. Multitasking is likely worse when doing complex, unfamiliar tasks such as studying.
- Think about how you can plan to reduce the effects of multitasking.

CHECK OUT THESE VIDEOS

The following are some great video resources on how to get the most out of studying:

1. Your authors Regan and John talking about key strategies: https://www.youtube.com/watch?v=Tp6yc96qNWU

2. Dr. Stephen Chew on studying: https://www.samford.edu/how-to-study/. Take note of the following videos in particular:
   - **Introductory Video (Optional):** Developing a Mindset for Successful Learning
   - **Video 1:** Beliefs That Make You Fail . . . Or Succeed
   - **Video 2:** What Students Should Understand About How People Learn
   - **Video 3:** Cognitive Principles for Optimizing Learning
   - **Video 4:** Putting the Principles for Optimizing Learning into Practice
   - **Video 5:** I Blew the Exam, Now What?

[Answer to Exercise 1: The even items are the best ones.]

GLOSSARY

Assessment: In general use, to assess is to measure, but in college it refers to the act of determining how well you are learning and what you have learned.

Calibration: The similarity between your judgment of how much you know, how well you did on a test of knowledge, and the actual test score.

Cramming: An ineffective practice schedule for producing long-term retention that involves studying to-be-learned material soon before (often the evening before) an upcoming exam.

Criterion learning: Continuing to study using practice retrieval (with feedback) until all material is correctly retrieved one time (i.e., a criterion of one correct retrieval), two times (i.e., a criterion of two correct retrievals), and so on.

Distributed practice: See **Spaced practice.**

Effect size: A statistical measure of how strong a role any single factor plays in research. Effect sizes (unlike correlations) can reach values higher than 1.0; the higher the effect, the stronger the part played by that factor. For example, class size has a medium effect size, suggesting that it is not as major an influence on learning as other factors.

Feeling of Knowing (FoK): Your understanding of and confidence in what you know, the accuracy of your knowledge, and what you do not know.

Interleaving: A practice schedule in which (a) different kinds of material are intermixed and practiced so (b) that the student does not know what kind of material they will be practicing next and hence first has to identify it. One example would involve intermixing different kinds of derivation problems in calculus so that, before deriving the solution to each problem, the student must first identify what kind of problem it is.

Massed practice: For a skill, practicing the same skill during a single session before moving on, without further practice of that skill; for studying, studying the same material in a single session. An example would be studying the definition of a concept for several minutes during a single study session without returning to study that definition again.

Metacognition: Commonly described as thinking about your thinking in relation to your learning, metacognition involves being consciously aware of yourself as a problem solver and the ability to accurately judge your own level of learning.

Meta-analysis: A form of research study or statistical analysis that combines the results of many different individual studies to provide a single measure of the strength of a particular effect or factor.

Monitoring: To evaluate—or monitor—how well you have learned something or how accurately you just answered a question. Taking a practice test is one way to help you monitor how well you have learned course material.

Retrieval practice: Attempting to retrieve information from your memory that you would like to learn; such practice can involve free recall (e.g., recall all you know about a topic), cued recall (a cue is provided, e.g., "What is the definition of covalent bonds?"), and answering multiple-choice questions, among others.

Self-explanation: Generating your own explanation for why a particular fact, concept, or way to solve a problem is correct.

Self-regulation: The process of paying attention to your learning process and, specifically, how you plan, monitor, and evaluate your performance.

Spaced practice: For a skill, practicing the same skill across multiple sessions spread across time; for studying, studying the same content (or material) across multiple sessions spread across time.

Study Champion: A person who successfully uses evidence-informed strategies to maximize their learning and practices diverse metacognitive skills.

Successive relearning: A technique that combines using retrieval practice with feedback until a criterion of (at least) one correct retrieval is met and then repeating this process again during one or more additional spaced-practice sessions.

Summarization: Generating the most important ideas about something (e.g., a text you have read, a video you watched, a lecture) in a relatively brief manner.

Transfer of learning: When the context of learning is different from the context of the eventual test. Examples include (a) practicing one geometry problem during study time and receiving a different version of that problem on an exam and (b) learning to solve fraction problems in a course on mathematics and then using that knowledge to increase the size of a recipe by one third.

Worked example: An example of a problem in which the solution is already worked out, providing all the steps required to solve it.

REFERENCES

Agarwal, P. K., Nunes, L. D., & Blunt, J. R. (2021). Retrieval practice consistently benefits student learning: A systematic review of applied research in schools and classrooms. *Educational Psychology Review*, *33*, 1409–1453. https://doi.org/10.1007/s10648-021-09595-9

Bain, K. (2012). *What the best college students do*. Belknap Press. https://doi.org/10.4159/harvard.9780674067479

Bartoszewski, B. L., & Gurung, R. A. R. (2015). Comparing the relationship of learning techniques and exam score. *Scholarship of Teaching and Learning in Psychology*, *1*(3), 219–228. https://doi.org/10.1037/stl0000036

Bernstein, D. A. (2018). Does active learning work? A good question, but not the right one. *Scholarship of Teaching and Learning in Psychology*, *4*(4), 290–307. https://doi.org/10.1037/stl0000124

Berry, D. C. (1983). Metacognitive experience and transfer of logical reasoning. *Quarterly Journal of Experimental Psychology*, *35*(1), 39–49. https://doi.org/10.1080/14640748308402115

Blasiman, R. N., Dunlosky, J., & Rawson, K. A. (2017). The what, how much, and when of study strategies: Comparing intended versus actual study behaviour. *Memory*, *25*(6), 784–792. https://doi.org/10.1080/09658211.2016.1221974

Burley, D. T., Anning, K. L., & van Goozen, S. H. M. (2022). The association between hyperactive behaviour and cognitive inhibition impairments in young children. *Child Neuropsychology*, *28*(3), 302–317. Advance online publication. https://doi.org/10.1080/09297049.2021.1976128

Butler, A. C. (2010). Repeated testing produces superior transfer of learning relative to repeated studying. *Journal of Experimental Psychology: Learning, Memory, and Cognition*, *36*(5), 1118–1133. https://doi.org/10.1037/a0019902

Callender, A. A., Franco-Watkins, A. M., & Roberts, A. S. (2016). Improving metacognition in the classroom through instruction, training, and feedback. *Metacognition and Learning*, *11*(2), 215–235. https://doi.org/10.1007/s11409-015-9142-6

Calma-Birling, D., & Gurung, R. A. R. (2017). Does a brief mindfulness intervention impact quiz performance? *Psychology Learning & Teaching*, *16*(3), 323–335. https://doi.org/10.1177/1475725717712785

Carver, C. S., & Connor-Smith, J. (2010). Personality and coping. *Annual Review of Psychology*, *61*, 679–704. https://doi.org/10.1146/annurev.psych.093008.100352

Centers for Disease Control and Prevention (2017). *Short sleep duration among US adults*. https://www.cdc.gov/sleep/data_statistics.html

Cepeda, N. J., Pashler, H., Vul, E., Wixted, J. T., & Rohrer, D. (2006). Distributed practice in verbal recall tasks: A review and quantitative synthesis. *Psychological Bulletin*, *132*(3), 354–380. https://doi.org/10.1037/0033-2909.132.3.354

Chen, P.-H. (2021). In-class and after-class lecture note-taking strategies. *Active Learning in Higher Education*, 22(3), 245–260. https://doi.org/10.1177/1469787419893490

Coutinho, S. A. (2007). The relationship between goals, metacognition, and academic success. *Educate*, 7(1), 39–47.

De Bruyckere, P., Kirschner, P. A., & Hulshof, C. D. (2015). *Urban myths about learning and education*. Elsevier/Academic Press.

Dunlosky, J., & Lipko, A. (2007). Metacomprehension: A brief history and how to improve its accuracy. *Current Directions in Psychological Science*, *16*(4), 228–232. https://doi.org/10.1111/j.1467-8721.2007.00509.x

Dunlosky, J., & O'Brien, A. (2020). The power of successive relearning and how to implement it with fidelity using pencil and paper and web-based programs. *Scholarship of Teaching and Learning in Psychology*. Advance online publication. https://doi.org/10.1037/stl0000233

Dunlosky, J., & Rawson, K. A. (Eds.). (2019). *The Cambridge handbook of cognition and education*. Cambridge University Press. https://doi.org/10.1017/9781108235631

Dunlosky, J., Rawson, K. A., Marsh, E. J., Nathan, M. J., & Willingham, D. T. (2013). Improving students' learning with effective learning techniques: Promising directions from cognitive and educational psychology. *Psychological Science in the Public Interest*, *14*(1), 4–58. https://doi.org/10.1177/1529100612453266

Dweck, C. S. (2007). *Mindset: The new psychology of success*. Ballantine.

Ebbinghaus, H. (1964). *Memory: A contribution to experimental psychology*. Dover. (Original work published 1885)

Einstein, G. O., Morris, J., & Smith, S. (1985). Note-taking, individual differences, and memory for lecture information. *Journal of Educational Psychology*, *77*(5), 522–532. https://doi.org/10.1037/0022-0663.77.5.522

Erblich, J. (2019). Alcohol use and health. In T. A. Revenson & R. A. R. Gurung (Eds.), *Handbook of health psychology* (pp. 133–147). Routledge.

Ertmer, P. A., & Newby, T. J. (1996). The expert learner: Strategic, self-regulated, and reflective. *Instructional Science*, *24*(1), 1–24. https://doi.org/10.1007/BF00156001

European Society of Cardiology. (2022, May 23). *Alcohol may be more risky to the heart than previously thought*. https://www.sciencedaily.com/releases/2022/05/220523135032.htm

Flavell, J. H. (1979). Metacognition and cognitive monitoring: A new area of cognitive–developmental inquiry. *American Psychologist*, *34*(10), 906–911. https://doi.org/10.1037/0003-066X.34.10.906

Foster, N. L., Was, C. A., Dunlosky, J., & Isaacson, R. M. (2017). Even after thirteen class exams, students are still overconfident: The role of memory for past exam performance in student predictions. *Metacognition and Learning*, *12*(1), 1–19. https://doi.org/10.1007/s11409-016-9158-6

Gallant, S. N. (2016). Mindfulness meditation practice and executive functioning: Breaking down the benefit. *Consciousness and Cognition*, *40*, 116–130. https://doi.org/10.1016/j.concog.2016.01.005

Gallup, Inc. (2014). *Great jobs, great lives: The 2014 Gallup–Purdue index report: A study of more than 30,000 college graduates across the U.S.* https://www.gallup.com/services/176768/2014-gallup-purdue-index-report.aspx

Gurung, R. A. R. (2014, September 3). Plan your crazy: A tip for the new school year. *Green Bay Press Gazette*. https://www.greenbaypressgazette.

com/story/news/education/2014/09/03/plan-crazy-tip-new-school-year/15037175

Gurung, R. A. R. (2016). *You a scapegoat? Answers to who's accountable for learning*. https://psychlearningcurve.org/scapegoat

Gurung, R. A. R. (2019). *Health psychology: Wellness in a diverse world*. Sage.

Gurung, R. A. R. (2020, February 13). RAP ON: Making metacognition visible. *Research Advancing Pedagogy*. https://blogs.oregonstate.edu/osuteaching/2020/02/13/rap-on-making-metacognition-visible

Gurung, R. A. R., & Burns, K. (2019). Putting evidence-based claims to the test: A multi-site classroom study of retrieval practice and spaced practice. *Applied Cognitive Psychology, 33*(5), 732–743. https://doi.org/10.1002/acp.3507

Gurung, R. A. R., & Galardi, N. R. (2021). Syllabus tone, more than mental health statements, influence intentions to seek help. *Teaching of Psychology*. Advance online publication. https://doi.org/10.1177/0098628321994632

Hacker, D. J., & Bol, L. (2019). Calibration and self-regulated learning: Making the connections. In J. Dunlosky & K. A. Rawson (Eds.), *The Cambridge handbook of cognition and education* (pp. 647–677). Cambridge University Press. https://doi.org/10.1017/9781108235631.026

Halliday, D. M., Epperson, A. E., & Song, A. V. (2019). Weight loss, obesity, and health. In T. A. Revenson & R. A. R. Gurung (Eds.), *Handbook of health psychology* (pp. 91–104). Routledge.

Hattie, J. (2015). The applicability of Visible Learning to higher education. *Scholarship of Teaching and Learning in Psychology, 1*(1), 79–91. https://doi.org/10.1037/stl0000021

Holliday, N. (2017, August 11). *Sydney Opera House failed project: What can you learn?* https://blog.beyondsoftware.com/learning-from-failed-projects-sydney-opera-house

Hong, W., Bernacki, M. L., & Perera, H. N. (2020). A latent profile analysis of undergraduates' achievement motivations and metacognitive behaviors, and their relations to achievement in science. *Journal of Educational Psychology, 112*(7), 1409–1430. https://doi.org/10.1037/edu0000445

Hoyt, L. T., Cohen, A. K., Dull, B., Maker Castro, E., & Yazdani, N. (2021). "Constant stress has become the new normal": Stress and anxiety inequalities among U.S. college students in the time of COVID-19. *Journal of Adolescent Health, 68*(2), 270–276. https://doi.org/10.1016/j.jadohealth.2020.10.030

James, W. (1890). *The principles of psychology: Vol. 2*. Henry Holt. https://doi.org/10.1037/11059-000

Kabat-Zinn, J. (2003). Mindfulness-based interventions in context: Past, present, and future. *Clinical Psychology: Science and Practice*, *10*(2), 144–156. https://doi.org/10.1093/clipsy/bpg016

Karat, C. M., Halverson, C., Horn, D., & Karat, J. (1999). Patterns of entry and correction in large vocabulary continuous speech recognition systems. In *CHI '99: Proceedings of the SIGCHI conference on human factors in computing systems* (pp. 568–575). Association for Computing Machinery. https://doi.org/10.1145/302979.303160

Komarraju, M., & Nadler, D. (2013). Self-efficacy and academic achievement: Why do implicit beliefs, goals, and effort regulation matter? *Learning and Individual Differences, 25*, 67–72. https://doi.org/10.1016/j.lindif.2013.01.005

Kruger, J., & Dunning, D. (1999). Unskilled and unaware of it: How difficulties in recognizing one's own incompetence lead to inflated self-assessments. *Journal of Personality and Social Psychology*, *77*(6), 1121–1134. https://doi.org/10.1037/0022-3514.77.6.1121

Lay, C. (1986). At last, my research article on procrastination. *Journal of Research in Personality*, *20*(4), 474–495. https://doi.org/10.1016/0092-6566(86)90127-3

Lieberman, D. E. (2021). *Exercised: Why something we never evolved to do is healthy and rewarding*. Pantheon.

Lipson, S. K., Lattie, E. G., & Eisenberg, D. (2019). Increased rates of mental health service utilization by U.S. college students: 10-year population-level trends (2007–2017). *Psychiatric Services, 70*(1), 60–63. https://doi.org/10.1176/appi.ps.201800332

Luo, L., Kiewra, K. A., & Samuelson, L. (2016). Revising lecture notes: How revision, pauses, and partners affect note taking and achievement. *Instructional Science*, *44*(1), 45–67. https://doi.org/10.1007/s11251-016-9370-4

Lutz, A., Slagter, H. A., Dunne, J. D., & Davidson, R. J. (2008). Attention regulation and monitoring in meditation. *Trends in Cognitive Sciences, 12*(4), 163–169. https://doi.org/10.1016/j.tics.2008.01.005

Mischel, W. (2014). *The Marshmallow Test: Mastering self-control.* Little, Brown.

Miyatsu, T., Nguyen, K., & McDaniel, M. A. (2018). Five popular study strategies: Their pitfalls and optimal implementations. *Perspectives on Psychological Science*, *13*(3), 390–407. https://doi.org/10.1177/1745691617710510

Morehead, K., Dunlosky, J., & Rawson, K. A. (2019). How much mightier is the pen than the keyboard for note-taking? A replication and extension of Mueller and Oppenheimer (2014). *Educational Psychology Review*, *31*(3), 753–780. https://doi.org/10.1007/s10648-019-09468-2

Morehead, K., Dunlosky, J., Rawson, K. A., Blasiman, R., & Hollis, R. B. (2019). Note-taking habits of 21st century college students: Implications for student learning, memory, and achievement. *Memory*, *27*(6), 807–819. https://doi.org/10.1080/09658211.2019.1569694

Morrison, A. B., Goolsarran, M., Rogers, S. L., & Jha, A. P. (2014). Taming a wandering attention: Short-form mindfulness training in student cohorts. *Frontiers in Human Neuroscience*, *7*, 897. https://doi.org/10.3389/fnhum.2013.00897

Mrazek, M. D., Franklin, M. S., Phillips, D. T., Baird, B., & Schooler, J. W. (2013). Mindfulness training improves working memory capacity and GRE performance while reducing mind wandering. *Psychological Science*, *24*(5), 776–781. https://doi.org/10.1177/0956797612459659

Mrazek, M. D., Smallwood, J., & Schooler, J. W. (2012). Mindfulness and mind-wandering: Finding convergence through opposing constructs. *Emotion*, *12*(3), 442–448. https://doi.org/10.1037/a0026678

Mueller, P. A., & Oppenheimer, D. M. (2014). The pen is mightier than the keyboard: Advantages of longhand over laptop note taking. *Psychological Science*, *25*(6), 1159–1168. https://doi.org/10.1177/0956797614524581

Paas, F. G. W. C., & van Merrienboer, J. G. (1994). Variability of worked examples and transfer of geometrical problem-solving skills: A cognitive-load approach. *Journal of Educational Psychology*, *86*(1), 122–133. https://doi.org/10.1037/0022-0663.86.1.122

Pashler, H., McDaniel, M., Rohrer, D., & Bjork, R. (2008). Learning styles: Concepts and evidence. *Psychological Science in the Public Interest*, *9*(3), 105–119. https://doi.org/10.1111/j.1539-6053.2009.01038.x

Pauk, W., & Ross, J. O. O. (2013). *How to study in college* (11th ed.). Cengage.

Peverly, S. T., & Wolf, A. D. (2019). Note-taking. In J. Dunlosky & K. A. Rawson (Eds.), *The Cambridge handbook of cognition and education* (pp. 320–355). Cambridge University Press. https://doi.org/10.1017/9781108235631.014

Pilcher, J. J., & Morris, D. M. (2020). Sleep and organizational behavior: Implications for workplace productivity and safety. *Frontiers in Psychology*, *11*, 45. https://doi.org/10.3389/fpsyg.2020.00045

Pinxten, M., De Laet, T., Van Soom, C., Peeters, C., & Langie, G. (2019). Purposeful delay and academic achievement. A critical review of the Active Procrastination Scale. *Learning and Individual Differences*, *73*, 42–51. https://doi.org/10.1016/j.lindif.2019.04.010

Pollan, M. (2007). *The omnivore's dilemma: A natural history of four meals*. Penguin.

Pomerance, L., Greenberg, J., & Walsh, K. (2016). *Learning about learning: What every new teacher needs to know*. National Council on Teaching Quality.

Putnam, A. L., Sungkhasettee, V. W., & Roediger, H. L., III. (2016). Optimizing learning in college: Tips from cognitive psychology. *Perspectives on Psychological Science*, *11*(5), 652–660. https://doi.org/10.1177/1745691616645770

Ragan, E. D., Jennings, S. R., Massey, J. D., & Doolittle, P. E. (2014). Unregulated use of laptops over time in large lecture classes. *Computers & Education, 78,* 78–86. https://doi.org/10.1016/j.compedu.2014.05.002

Ramsburg, J. T., & Youmans, R. J. (2014). Meditation in the higher-education classroom: Meditation training improves student knowledge retention during lectures. *Mindfulness*, *5*(4), 431–441. https://doi.org/10.1007/s12671-013-0199-5

Raver, S. A., & Maydosz, A. S. (2010). Impact of the provision and timing of instructor-provided notes on university students' learning. *Active Learning in Higher Education, 11*(3), 189–200. https://doi.org/10.1177/1469787410379682

Rawson, K. A., Dunlosky, J., & Sciartelli, S. M. (2013). The power of successive relearning: Improving performance on course exams and long-term retention. *Educational Psychology Review*, *25*(4), 523–548. https://doi.org/10.1007/s10648-013-9240-4

Rawson, K. A., & Kintsch, W. (2005). Rereading effects depend on time of test. *Journal of Educational Psychology*, *97*(1), 70–80. https://doi.org/10.1037/0022-0663.97.1.70

Robbins, S. B., Lauver, K., Le, H., Davis, D., Langley, R., & Carlstrom, A. (2004). Do psychosocial and study skill factors predict college outcomes? A meta-analysis. *Psychological Bulletin*, *130*(2), 261–288. https://doi.org/10.1037/0033-2909.130.2.261

Robles, T. F., Mercado, E., Nooteboom, P., Price, J., & Romney, C. (2019). Biological processes of health. In T. A. Revenson & R. A. R. Gurung (Eds.), *Handbook of health psychology* (pp. 69–88). Routledge.

Roediger, H. L., III, Putnam, A. L. O., & Smith, M. A. (2011). Ten benefits of testing and their applications to educational practice. *Psychology of Learning and Motivation*, *55*, 1–36. https://doi.org/10.1016/B978-0-12-387691-1.00001-6

Rohrer, D., Dedrick, R. F., Hartwig, M. K., & Cheung, C. (2020). A randomized controlled trial of interleaved mathematics practice. *Journal of Educational Psychology*, *112*(1), 40–52. https://doi.org/10.1037/edu0000367

Schraw, G. (1998). Promoting general metacognition awareness. *Instructional Science*, *26*(1-2), 113–125. https://doi.org/10.1023/A:1003044231033

Schraw, G., & Dennison, R. S. (1994). Assessing metacognitive awareness. *Contemporary Educational Psychology*, *19*(4), 460–475. https://doi.org/10.1006/ceps.1994.1033

Senzaki, S., Hackathorn, J., Appleby, D. C., & Gurung, R. A. R. (2017). Reinventing flashcards to increase student learning. *Psychology Learning & Teaching*, *16*(3), 353–368. https://doi.org/10.1177/1475725717719771

Tanner, K. D. (2012). Promoting student metacognition. *CBE Life Sciences Education*, *11*(2), 113–120. https://doi.org/10.1187/cbe.12-03-0033

Taraban, R., Maki, W. S., & Rynearson, K. (1999). Measuring study time distributions: Implications for designing computer-based courses. *Behavior Research Methods, Instruments & Computers*, *31*(2), 263–269. https://doi.org/10.3758/BF03207718

Thomas, R. C., Weywadt, C. R., Anderson, J. L., Martinez-Papponi, B., & McDaniel, M. A. (2018). Testing encourages transfer between factual and application questions in an online learning environment. *Journal of Applied Research in Memory and Cognition*, 7(2), 252–260. https://doi.org/10.1016/j.jarmac.2018.03.007

Troisi, J. D., & Gabriel, S. (2011). Chicken soup really is good for the soul: "Comfort food" fulfills the need to belong. *Psychological Science, 22*(6), 747–753. https://doi.org/10.1177/0956797611407931

Urry, H. L., Crittle, C. S., Floerke, V. A., Leonard, M. Z., Perry, C. S., III, Akdilek, N., Albert, E. R., Block, A. J., Bollinger, C. A., Bowers, E. M., Brody, R. S., Burk, K. C., Burnstein, A., Chan, A. K., Chan, P. C., Chang, L. J., Chen, E., Chiarawongse, C. P., Chin, G., . . . Zarrow, J. E. (2021). Don't ditch the laptop just yet: A direct replication of Mueller and Oppenheimer's (2014) Study 1 plus mini meta-analyses across similar studies. *Psychological Science, 32*(3), 326–339. https://doi.org/10.1177/0956797620965541

U.S. Department of Agriculture & U.S. Department of Health and Human Services. (2020, December). *Dietary guidelines for Americans, 2020–2025* (9th ed.). https://www.dietaryguidelines.gov/resources/2020-2025-dietary-guidelines-online-materials

U.S. Department of Health and Human Services. (2018). *Physical activity guidelines for Americans* (2nd ed.). https://health.gov/sites/default/files/2019-09/Physical_Activity_Guidelines_2nd_edition.pdf

van Gog, T., Rummel, N., & Renkl, A. (2019). Learning how to solve problems by studying examples. In J. Dunlosky & K. A. Rawson (Eds.), *The Cambridge handbook of cognition and education* (pp. 183–208). Cambridge University Press. https://doi.org/10.1017/9781108235631.009

Wang, A. Y., Thomas, M. H., & Ouellette, J. A. (1992). Keyword mnemonic and retention of second-language vocabulary words. *Journal of Educational Psychology, 84*(4), 520–528. https://doi.org/10.1037/0022-0663.84.4.520

Waters, L., Barsky, A., Ridd, A., & Allen, K. (2015). Contemplative education: A systematic, evidence-based review of the effect of meditation interventions in schools. *Educational Psychology Review, 27*(1), 103–134. https://doi.org/10.1007/s10648-014-9258-2

Weinstein, Y., Madan, C. R., & Sumeracki, M. A. (2018). Teaching the science of learning. *Cognitive Research: Principles and Implications, 3*(1), 2. https://doi.org/10.1186/s41235-017-0087-y

Wiseheart, M., Küpper-Tetzel, C. E., Weston, T., Kim, A. S. N., Kapler, I. V., & Foot-Seymour, V. (2019). Enhancing the quality of student learning using distributed practice. In J. Dunlosky & K. A. Rawson (Eds.),

The Cambridge handbook of cognition and education (pp. 550–584). Cambridge University Press.

Wong, L. (2014). *Essential study skills* (8th ed.). Cengage Learning.

Yamada, K., & Victor, T. L. (2012). The impact of mindful awareness practices on college student health, well-being, and capacity for learning: A pilot study. *Psychology Learning & Teaching*, *11*(2), 139–145. https://doi.org/10.2304/plat.2012.11.2.139

Zeigler, D. W., Wang, C. C., Yoast, R. A., Dickinson, B. D., McCaffree, M. A., Robinowitz, C. B., Sterling, M. L.; Council on Scientific Affairs, American Medical Association. (2005). The neurocognitive effects of alcohol on adolescents and college students. *Preventive Medicine*, *40*(1), 23–32. https://doi.org/10.1016/j.ypmed.2004.04.044

Zimmerman, B. J. (2008). Investigating self-regulation and motivation: Historical background, methodological developments, and future prospects. *American Educational Research Journal*, *45*(1), 166–183. https://doi.org/10.3102/0002831207312909

INDEX

ABOUT THE AUTHORS

Regan A. R. Gurung, PhD, is a social psychologist by training and conducts research encompassing social, health, and pedagogical psychology. He has had more than 120 articles published in peer-reviewed journals and has coauthored or coedited 15 books. His most recent book is *Thriving in Academia* (with Mark E. Basham and Pamela I. Ansburg). He is the founding coeditor of the American Psychological Association's (APA's) journal *Scholarship of Teaching and Learning in Psychology*; cochaired the APA General Psychology Initiative; and is currently past president of Psi Chi, the International Honor Society in Psychology. At Oregon State University, he is associate vice provost and executive director of the Center for Teaching and Learning, professor of psychological science, and director of the General Psychology Program. Dr. Gurung taught at the University of Wisconsin–Green Bay (UWGB) for 20 years before moving to Corvallis, Oregon, in 2019. While at UWGB, he served in many different roles, including associate dean of the College of Arts, Humanities, and Social Sciences; department chair of Human Development; codirector of the university's Teaching Scholars Program; and on the University of Wisconsin System's Office of Professional Development Executive Committee. He has consulted with and conducted workshops at numerous teaching and learning centers both nationally and internationally.

John Dunlosky, PhD, is a professor in the Department of Psychological Sciences and the director of the Science of Learning and Education Center at Kent State University. He is keenly interested in understanding students' metacognition and self-regulated learning, and his research focuses on discovering techniques that students can use to improve their learning and achievement. Along with long-time collaborator Dr. Katherine Rawson, Dr. Dunlosky has been conducting research involving real classrooms to evaluate and improve the impact of successive relearning, which is arguably one of the most effective strategies for gaining and obtaining mastery in any domain. He also coauthored the first textbook on metacognition and has edited several volumes on education, including the *Cambridge Handbook of Cognition and Education* and *Metacognition in Educational Theory and Practice.*